A brief history of Greece
1941-1949

Other books from D.T. Karamitsos

Medical

1. Σακχαρώδης Διαβήτης. Παθογένεια, Διάγνωση, Θεραπεία, Επιπλοκαί. Εκδ. Αλ. Σιώκης, Θεσσαλονίκη 1976.
2. Σακχαρώδης Διαβήτης (φοιτητικές σημειώσεις). Εκδ. Univ. Studio Press, Θεσσαλονίκη 1986.
3. Σακχαρώδης Διαβήτης. Από τη θεωρία στην πράξη. Εκδ. Αλ. Σιώκης, Θεσσαλονίκη 1987.
4. Διαβητολογία. Θεωρία και πρακτική στην αντιμετώπιση του σακχαρώδη διαβήτη. Εκδ. Σιώκης, Θεσσαλονίκη 2000.
5. Κλινική εξέταση και διάγνωση (επιμ. μετά των Μ. Σιών και Γ. Γιαννόγλου). Εκδ. Univ. Studio Press, Θεσσαλονίκη 2007.
6. Διαβητολογία. Θεωρία και πρακτική στην αντιμετώπιση του σακχαρώδη διαβήτη. 2η αναθεωρημένη έκδοση. Εκδ. Σιώκης, Αθήνα 2009.

Non Medical

1. Χρονογραφήματα ενός γιατρού. Εκδ. Univ. Studio Press, Θεσσαλονίκη 2001.
2. Η πόλη μας κι εμείς άλλοτε και τώρα. Θεσσαλονίκη 1941-2005. Εκδ. University Studio Press, Θεσσαλονίκη 2005.
3. Οικογένεια Μπαρλαμπά (Μυθιστόρημα). Εκδ. University Studio Press, Θεσσαλονίκη 2010.
4. Ιστορία της νεότερης Ελλάδας. Πολιτική και στρατιωτική. Α΄ τόμος 1897-1941. Εκδ. University Studio Press, Θεσσαλονίκη 2016.
5. Ιστορία της νεότερης Ελλάδας. Πολιτική και στρατιωτική. Β΄ τόμος 1942-1967. Εκδ. University Studio Press, Θεσσαλονίκη 2017.

Persons appeared at the cover of this book

King George B', J. Metaxas, A. Papagos

G. Tsolakoglou, E. Tsouderos, S. Venizelos, G. Papandreou

N. Plastiras, P. Kanellopoulos, T. Sofoulis, K. Tsaldaris

King Paul, Queen Frederica, T. Tsakalotos

N. Zachariadis, G. Siantos, M. Vafiadis, S. Sarafis

Dimitrios T. Karamitsos

A brief history of Greece
1941 – 1949

International Hellenic Association

A brief history of Greece: 1941-1949
by
Dimitrios T. Karamitsos
Professor emeritus
Aristotle University
Thessaloniki, Greece

This is an edition for the
International Hellenic Association
Via AMAZON

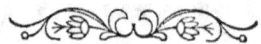

Blog: dtkaram.webpages.auth.gr

Facebook: Dimitrios Karamitsos

e-mail: dtkarami@yahoo.gr

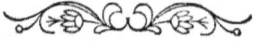

The present book is dealing
with the years 1941-1949
based on my book in the Greek language
under the title
History of modern Greece
(Ιστορία της νεότερης Ελλάδας-
Πολιτική και στρατιωτική)
Α΄ Volume 1897-1941
Β΄ Volume 1942-1967
Edited by University Studio Press
info@universitystudiopress.gr
blog: www.universitystudiopress.gr

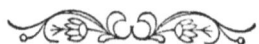

On the dawn of the new decade 2020

This book is dedicated
to the succeeding generations;

That
They must forgive,
Yet they must not forget
For not repeating the former tragedies.

Acknowledgments

I ought to thank four people that they helped me to improve the English language that I had used in the draft text:

Mrs. Despina Anastasiadis-Karamitsos, Teatcher of English language

Prof. Kyriakos Anastasiadis, head of Medical School, Aristotle University, Thessaloniki

Prof. Antonios Andreatos, Professor, Computer Engineering Division, Hellenic Air Force Academy

Prof. Nina Gatzoulis, Adjunct Professor of Modern Greek at the University of New Hampshire and Director of the Modern Greek Studies Program

CONTENTS

Preface 11
Acronyms and Initials 13
Chapter 1. An introduction for the events
 prior to the occupation 15
Chapter 2. The triple occupation of Greece........................ 19
Chapter 3. The national resistance 1941-1944 29
Chapter 4. The liberation of Greece 93
Chapter 5. The government instability: 1944-1947............... 115
Chapter 6. The civil war 1946-1949 129
- The prelude - Guerrillas against the Greek State 129
- Events of 1947 137
- Events of 1948 144
- Events of 1949 153

Epilogue... 179
Literature 182

PREFACE

This book focuses on the turbulent period of Greek history from 1941 to 1949. Its beginning includes the Greek National Resistance that developed in Greece against the three Occupation Forces; Germany, Italy, and Bulgaria. Subsequently, there are three successive phases of a bloody civil war from 1943 to 1949, when the communists fought against the Anti-communists and the Greek state. Those years left indelible traces of blood and lamentation in almost every Greek family, while the consequences were in overall tragic: many dead and injured people, lots of burned villages in the countryside and infrastructure irreversibly damaged.

Inevitably, there are a lot of serious questions that arise from these events: Why there was so much hatred among political parties and social classes? Why did this scary bloodshed happen? Why Greeks fought against each other? Why Greeks were entrapped to this national schism? Why Greeks make the same mistakes repeatedly throughout their history?

I believe that the knowledge of our history is a key so as the succeeding generations avoid the mistakes of their ancestors and prevent our nation's disunity in the future.

My main aim is to offer to Greeks who live abroad —especially the second generation— an opportunity to learn what happened in that critical period of Greek history.

1-8-2020

Dimitrios T. Karamitsos
Professor Emeritus
Aristotle University
Thessaloniki, Greece

ACRONYMS and INITIALS

DA (Democratic Army, an army of the KKE guerrillas 1946-1949)

EAM (National Liberation Front, a resistance organization with leftist leaders)

EAO (National Resistance Organization, Anton Tsaous groups)

EDES (National Republican Greek League, Napoleon Zervas group)

EES (Greek National Army, a league of anti-kommounists in Macedonia)

EKKA (National and Social Liberation, D. Psarros group)

ELAS (National Popular Liberation Army, A. Velouchiotis, S. Sarafis, A.Tzimas resistance group)

NA (National Army, the army of the Greek state)

OPLA (People's Struggle Protection Organization)

PEAN (Panhellenic Union of Fighting Youths, leader K. Perrikos)

SBs (Security Battalions)

SOE (Security Operations Executive, the British anti-spy organization)

USSR (Union of Socialistic Soviet Democracies)

YBE (Defenders of Northern Greece, a resistance group in Macedonia)

PAO (Panellenic Resistance Organization, a resistance group, evolution of YBE)

Note: The acronyms and initials for Greek parties and organization are based in Greek onomatology.

Chapter 1

AN INTRODUCTION OF THE EVENTS PRIOR TO THE OCCUPATION

Europe in the B´ world war

Germany joined Austria in 1938 (Germany terminology = Anschluss) and allied with Italy. Germany and Italy those days were ruled by dictatorial national socialists, Hitler and Mussolini respectively. Germany easily conquered Czechoslovakia (1938), and after securing the neutrality of the Soviet Union (through the German-Soviet Non-Attack Pact of August 1939), began World War II with the invasion of Poland on the 1st of September 1939. Britain and France soon responded by declaring war on Germany, but Hitler easily conquered most of Western Europe without difficulty (Netherlands, Belgium, Denmark, and France). The German army was then preparing to invade the USSR (Union of Socialistic Soviet Democracies) despite the Non-Attack Pact.

Dictatorship in Greece by John Metaxas

On August 4, 1936, the Greek Prime Minister General J. Metaxas suspended some articles of the Greek Constitution, thus establishing a dictatorial government without the functioning of the Parliament. King George B' of Greece was in agreement with the Prime Minister on this political change. The official excuse for the dictatorship was a danger for the security of the state because of the Communistic Party of Greece (KKE) actions e.g. an impending general strike. The Metaxas government organized the state to gain self-sufficiency in food, reinforced the army, built many fortifications on the border with Bulgaria, stimulated national youth thinking through the National Youth Organization (EON), implemented the State Security Institute (IKA) for the population's health care and social security and took some other measures to support poor people and farmers of the country. The dictatorial government thwarted communist propaganda and displaced many communists in small Aegean islands.

Greece defended its territory against two opponents

On October 28, 1940, the Italian Ambassador Grazzi delivered an ultimatum to Prime Minister Metaxas at 3:00 am; Italy wanted to seize certain parts of the country that were of strategic importance. In the case of Greece's denial, according to the ultimatum, Italy was ready to invade Greek territory at 6:00 am. Metaxas rejected promptly the ultimatum and his decision remained in Greek history as a big «NO».

The Greek army defended itself well and after eight days —thanks to successful army mobilization— began a counterattack and Greek Army pushed the Italians several kilometers out of the borders deeply into Albania. The war was hard, mainly mountainous, in very low temperatures, thus many soldiers had suffered from frozen legs causing gangrene. At the end of January J. Metaxas died after 10 days of febrile illness from peritonsillar abscess. King George appointed soon Al. Korizis (he was a banker) as Prime Minister. In March 1941 the Greeks managed to repel a major attack in which the Italian dictator Mussolini himself was present in Albania. The victories of Greece over Italy were the first victories of a state on the side of the British and French allies who until then had a hard time fighting the mighty German army. The British Prime Minister

1. An Introduction of the Events prior to the Occupation

Winston Churchill had congratulated publicly the Greek People for it successful defense against Italy.

On April 6, 1941, the 12th German army corps (680,000 men, 1,200 tanks, and 1,400 planes (600 planes especially for Greece) attacked Yugoslavia and Greece. The attack against Greek territory took place from the Bulgarian border, where there were strong forts (mainly underground) of the so-called «Metaxas Line». At the same time, the Germans attacked Yugoslavia; they conquered it very quickly and reached Thessaloniki two days later without difficulty, because Greece at the border with Yugoslavia did not have sufficient forces to defend itself. The Greek army at the Greek-Bulgarian border inevitably had to capitulate with Germans locally despite the fact that defended quite successfully thanks to the strong «Metaxas Line». Inevitably a local capitulation has been agreed. The Greek army in Albania would have already been between two enemies (Italians from the north and Germans from the South and East), so General Tsolakoglou, the leader of the 3rd Army Corp in Ioannina, decided to capitulate initially with Germans and then with the Italians disobeying to both King George and Major General A. Papagos in Athens (Papagos was the chief General military commander of Greece) who refused to capitulate. However, Tsolakoglou insisted and finally signed the capitulation. According to this capitulation, the Greek army would not be considered captive. General Tsolakoglou would soon take over as Prime Minister of a government of limited capabilities without a minister of the Exterior affairs.

On the 18th of April in Athens, Prime Minister Korizis commited swicide and King George appointed as the new Prime Minister Emmanuel Tsouderos, but soon the new government as well and the King went to Crete to continue the war against AXIS. In Crete Major-General Bernard Freyberg, a New-Zealand Army officer, was appointed commander of the local Allied forces. On the 20th of May 1941 strong German forces attacked Crete, mainly by air using many paratroopers.

The air force that attacked the island consisted of: 328 bombers, 205 vertical attacking Stucas, 233 Pursuers, 530 Transporter aircraft and 50 Gliders. The defenders were British, New Zealanders and Australians (The British Commonwealth contingent consisted of the original 14,000-men British garrison and another 25,000 British and Commonwealth troops that were evacuated from the mainland) along with Greek soldiers (about 9,000 men). The German troops encountered also mass resistance from the civilian population and gendarmes. The defenders had lacked in heavy equipment, planes, and armored vehicles. The Germans occupied the island after 10 days of tough battles but had many losses and dead paratroopers (57%). King George and the Prime Minister E. Tsouderos left Crete and were transported to Egypt under adventurous conditions. The gold of the Bank of Greece was shipped safely to South Africa.

Chapter 2

THE TRIPLE OCCUPATION OF GREECE

The Occupation circumstances

Three military forces were deployed in Greece: Germans, Italians, and Bulgarians. Bulgaria was not involved in battles with Greece but allied with Germany. After General Tsolakoglou capitalized, the Greek state would be operating with limited jurisdictions and capabilities. Ministries, Prefectures, Municipalities, and Communities, (except the Ministry of Foreign Affairs) maintained the administrative structure of the country. The Gendarmerie and the Police were also kept intact. Tsolakoglou's cabinet consisted mainly of military personnel. Two diplomats, German Altenburg and Italian Ghigi were designated as Governors of Greece. Additionally, the Austrian Lieutenant General Löhr was vested the military authority in Greece.

The conquerors felt relief since a large occupation army would not be needed in Greece. However, the country's infrastructure was damaged by the bombing. There were no roads or any other ways of safe transportation. The Greek soldiers who returned after the war to Athens and Thessaloniki were still wearing their ragged military uniforms. The German officers were settled in nice detached houses by evicting their owners or limiting them to the worst rooms of their houses.

The German authorities swiftly exploited the country's wealthy resources. They confiscated all the food that was in the warehouses for the nourishment of the occupying troops; this referred mainly to legumes, vegetables, olive oils, raisins, and figs. The leftovers, like canned sardines, were the only eatables offered to Greeks and obviously they were quickly consumed. Moreover, the Germans confiscated all the stored tobacco. In the following years, the Occupation Authorities generally had retained arbitrarily 10-35% of the various agricultural products.

The Germans, also arbitrarily, set the exchange rate of the German mark to drachma at 1 to 60, while they printed German marks were distributed to their soldiers. As a result, the German soldiers were able to render the Greek shops out of stock. Furthermore, the German weapon company «Krupp» was empowered to exploit all the Greek ore mines (chromium, bauxite, manganese, nickel). Bodossakis' factories (ammunition production and equipment) were transferred to Germany. Telefunken obtained a monopoly on radio and telegraphy. Hansa Leichtmetall took over the water resources exploitation, Lufthansa operated the air transportation and Südostropa obtained the monopoly of the silk production. The Italians were surprised by the agility and efficiency of the Germans to manipulate the Greek resources and managed to take advantage of the situation as well.

However, Greece was blocked by the British navy so that Germans could not get supplies easily, and as a result, hunger prevailed to the Greeks, especially in Athens. Similarly, wheat transportation from Macedonia and Thessaly to Athens became extremely difficult due to damaged roads. Another difficulty in transportation was due to the division of the country into three regions with borders controlled by the Occupation Armies and the different currencies used in them. Thus, the average calorie consumption per worker was only 875 Kcal per day, and hence people were losing on average 9-11 pounds per month. Consequently, many Greeks died of starvation in the winter of 1942, especially in Athens. A ship called «Kurtuluş» made five trips to Greece carrying food aid from Turkey, endorsed by the Inter-

2. The Triple Occupation of Greece

national Red Cross (IRC). However, it eventually sank (probably by the British) and thereafter this humanitarian relief ceased. The United Kingdom decided in February 1942 (after a delayed decision by the British Parliament) to exclude Greece from the naval blockade and then allowed the Swedish Red Cross to deliver food aid; such a grave situation, however, was far from getting recovered. Thus, many citizens, especially in big cities and mostly in Athens, suffered from low body proteins. Their bellies filled with fluid and also they had ended up with swollen feet. Many started fainting and dying in the streets.

Table 1:
Declared deaths in Athens, 1940-1945 (by month and year)[1]

	1940	1941	1942	1943	1944	1945
January	690	807	3096	971	856	916
February	547	650	2802	765	861	1192
March	727	733	2738	766	721	926
April	572	683	1899	592	713	789
May	644	708	1467	538	722	814
June	606	753	1316	601	819	694
July	635	716	1417	790	912	722
August	544	729	1143	543	962	686
September	502	853	1032	483	841	574
October	536	1089	1259	630	772	633
November	546	1677	1294	604	697	608

1 Hatzimichael Y. Demographics of Athens during the period 1940-1945. Postgraduate diploma thesis at the Department of History and Archeology of the University of Crete, Rethymnon 2000.

December	760	3613	1070	708	398	662
TOTAL	**7309**	**13011**	**20533**	**7991**	**9274**	**9216**

The International Red Cross (IRC) had estimated that the famine deaths were about 250,000 during that period. This means that more Greeks died of starvation than from bullets during the war. It is necessary to note that due to the assistance of the IRC the average daily calorie intake of Greeks rose to 1,300 Kcal, yet this was still insufficient. To put this intake into a medical perspective, 1,300 Kcal is the current recommendation for weight loss. The Germans and the Italians were willing to cooperate with the IRC in the effort to deliver food aid. This was due to their interest in avoiding resistance movements that could be enhanced by hunger. Additionally, various patriotic organizations, as well as the Greek Church, supported poor people by organizing fundraisers and providing food.

Unfortunately, due to food shortage, many market traders took advantage of the situation by hiding food and then selling it at high prices to the so-called «black market». Especially olive oil became extremely overpriced. Germans tried to stop the black market. There is an example of two olive oil merchants who were sentenced to death by hanging because they had hidden olive oil. However, the overall number of black-market dealers was overwhelming. Purchases were mostly made in gold pounds because the banknotes were of no value due to the extremely high inflation rate. Additionally, bread supply was inadequate. In fact, the bread price was 10 drachmas in 1941; however, due to the deficient supply and the high inflation rate, its price reached 153 million drachmas in 1944. In general, due to starvation many citizens were forced to sell their property to the black-market traders. Death by starvation had risen to an unprecedented level and mostly affecting the inferior economic classes.

2. The Triple Occupation of Greece

On the 14th March 1942, Altenburg and Ghigi signed a loan agreement, which was later announced to the Hellenic State in a verbatim report. According to the agreement: the Greek government would be obliged to pay a holding fee of 1.5 billion drachmas per month, withdrawals from the Bank of Greece over this amount would be granted to the governments of Germany and Italy as an interest-free loan from Greece. The loan would be paid off later, while the agreement would have retrospective effect from 1st January 1942. It is interesting that the loan was interest-free and in drachmas, yet it was mandatory. Loan withdrawals would have taken the form of monthly advances, their amount and duration however, is still to be determined; similarly, it was unclear when those loans would be paid off. It is important to mention that until now (in 2020) this load has not been settled. Prime Minister Tsolakoglou resigned at the end of 1942, and Logothetopoulos, who was Professor of Gynaecology, the Vice-President and the Minister of Health, succeeded him as the Prime Minister. In October of 1942, the German politician Hermann Neubacher arrived in Greece to assist in financial affairs. He reduced the banknotes and sold the gold (seized by the Jews of Thessaloniki) to the Greek Stock Exchange, in order to strengthen the drachma. He then managed to improve the living conditions of city residents while fighting the profiteering Greek merchants and industrialists. In some cases, Neubacher's arrangement protected the Greeks from the arbitrariness of the Occupation Authorities. However, as time passed, black-market re-emerged, and the drachma value was completely lost. As a result of this situation, many civilians towards the end of the Occupation in 1944, simply exchanged products with each other since this was much more efficient.

Altenburg and Neubacher tried to aid the occupied country administratively, but obviously, their main interest was Germany and the German army. On the 7th of April 1943, the conservative politician John Rallis succeeded Logothetopoulos as the Prime Minister of Greece and remained in this post until the 12th of October 1944. In order to accept the position, Rallis demanded from Germans the fulfillment of two conditions: the prohibition of the Bulgarians movement toward Thessaloniki and the establishment of the Security Battalions (SBs). Both of these conditions were satisfied. In Rallis's administration a few supporters of dead politician El. Venizelos (Liberals party) participated.

During the Occupation, a major strike took place to prevent the major exploitation of Greeks by Germans who wanted Greeks not only to work for them but also to fight for them. In February 1943, General Speidel issued an order stating: «All 16-45 years old men are obliged to carry out the duties that have appointed by the German or Italian services». It is noted that in 1941 only 550 Greeks were registered workers in Germany, compared to 109,000 Yugoslavs and 14,600 Bulgarians. During those protests, Logothetopoulos' office was burned by protesters and later the Ministry of Labour was broken, and several documents were burned. Moreover, there were several collisions with the Carabineer forces resulting in 18 dead and 135 wounded protesters. Archbishop Damaskinos visited Altenburg to inform him the Church's opposition to his intention of recruiting Greeks. His intervention was successful and hence peace was announced. Already a «battle» against Nazi Germany had been won.

It is worth to write that the old politicians during the occupation's years spent their time by conducting «academic» debates about what would happen after the end of the war, as well as about several issues that had been risen by the King's involvement to Metaxas's dictatorship.

2. The Triple Occupation of Greece

The Bulgarian Occupation in Macedonia and Thrace

In 1941, the Germans granted the administration of certain parts of the country to Bulgarians: Eastern Macedonia and Thrace, except from one strip of land in the eastern borders, that was kept by Germans. However, the Germans did not regard this territory as an «attachment» to Bulgaria, as was the case with the Ionian Islands which were under the Italian occupation. The Germans had promised to resolve the issue after the war.

Bulgarians moved all factories, machinery, and food from the Greek land to Bulgaria. They forbade local farmers to store wheat, corn, and oil and forced them to report their production and deliver it to the Bulgarian administration. The villagers would then only get bread from state ovens using vouchers. In grocery stores, butchers and fish shops signs were placed: «only for Bulgarians» as separate food vouchers and possibilities were provided for them. Food, and especially meat, was supplied with low tax only to those who had Bulgarian names, while the Greeks were taxed in double. Greeks could pay fewer taxes only if they had a Bulgarian partner!

The Bulgarians attempted to disturb Greek social life. For example, only Bulgarian doctors could handle medicines, so patients had to contact exclusively a Bulgarian doctor. Moreover, the Bulgarian authorities banned Greek newspapers and magazines. All Greek firms, both state and private, had to become Bulgarian. They founded a Bulgarian Club in Thessaloniki where young people received a gift of 1,000 levas and they could study for free in Sofia upon registration. Without Bulgarian documents, Greeks were not allowed to travel within the country. Moreover, the Bulgarians closed the Greek schools and expelled the teachers, replacing them with Bulgarian teachers, and they also burned Greek school books.

Furthermore, it was even forbidden to paint houses in blue, since that color was a reminder of the Greek flag.

In order to contact the Administration, Greeks had to speak in Bulgarian language. In the villages, several offices were installed where Bulgarian military officers registered the citizens to either Greek or Bulgarian; the latter gained privileges. Specifically, the accepted the Bulgarian citizenship they appointed as mail carriers, teachers, priests, community presidents, community secretaries, messengers, civil servants, gendarmes, guards, rural constables and so on. Anyone who responded that he or she was Greek suffered harsh consequences on various occasions. The Bulgarians also changed the names of those who identified themselves as «Bulgarians», so that they would look Bulgarian. This was done by adding the ending/suffix «of» to their family names. Moreover, together with the Bulgarian army, thousands of Bulgarian villagers arrived in Eastern Macedonia, with horse-drawn wagons and were settled in the confiscated homes of Greeks.

From the very first days of the Bulgarian occupation, many Greek civilians were deported. They also sent Greeks to Bulgaria in Labour Battalions, where they were forced to do heavy manual work and for that they were paid with a small amount of Bulgarian banknotes. Bulgarians terrorized the villagers by announcing that if any of them try to revolt against them, there would be retaliatory executions of hostages.

The provocation of the rebellion in Drama

On the 28th of September 1941, several attacks were carried out by Greek armed men at the community offices and police stations of 16 municipalities in the region of Drama. The residents were urged to join the rebels. The village Doxato was the place where the first attack began resulting in an injury of the Bulgarian Prefect. Many nearby villages were also attacked.

2. The Triple Occupation of Greece

The responsibility for the attacks was attributed to the local organization of the KKE (Communist Greek Party), following the propaganda of Bulgarian agents, who appeared as communists who alleged the «communist insurrection in the Balkans». Subsequently, the Bulgarian army killed a lot of those people who had not agreed to be considered Bulgarians. After these events, it is estimated that around 10,000 Greeks moved to the German-occupied areas for their own safety. The total number of dead Greeks from the Bulgarian atrocities is estimated at 15,000, out of which, 238 were executed in Doxato.

In 1943, the Bulgarians wanted to expand their area of occupation to Thessaloniki. As a result, on the 13th and 23rd of July 1941, several resistance groups organized major protests in Athens, where 22 protesters died, and many others were injured. The Hellenic Prime Minister expressed to Germans its dissatisfaction on this Bulgarian attempt. Ultimately, the impending Bulgarian expansion was prevented. In response to the aims of the Bulgarians, Greek Macedonians founded the «Macedonian and Thracian Society», in which among others Professor Al. Svolos, the politician K. Karamanlis and the General Governor of Macedonia Colonel Chrysochoou participated.

The total number of Greeks who had been exiled or who had decided to flee voluntarily from the Bulgarian-occupied areas was estimated finally it was 200,000 people. Rich Greeks were blackmailed by Bulgarian officers that were pressing them to give their belongings to them in exchange for their «protection»! In March 1943 the Bulgarians implemented the German Nazi program and they captured about 9,000 Jews from their occupying territory and sent them to concentration camps. In fact, many Greek Jews were loaded to boats in the Danube heading to Wien. Unfortunately, all boats sank with no survivors (obviously, they were drowned on purpose)! From the 9,000 Jews only 70 managed to return home after the war.

The Italian Occupation

The Germans directed most of the country's administration to the Italians. At first, the Italian authorities were particularly harsh with the Greeks because they were irritated by their heroic battles in the mountains of Albania. Moreover, they had already attempted the de-Hellenization of some parts of the country, such as the Dodecanese, which Italy had already owned since 1912, and the Ionian Islands, where it was compulsory the use of the Italian language in public services and education. The Italians also imposed the Italian law into courts. Furthermore, in order to impose themselves on the Ionian Islands, they arrested and relocated 3,500 Greeks to concentration camps. On Pindos mountain, Italians organized the so-called 5th Roman Legion and tried to create the «Principality of Pindos» headed by the so-called «Prince-Ruler» (!) Alcibiadis Diamantis, a Vlach lawyer born in Samarina village, (see in the special chapter).

The economy of Greece in the areas controlled by the Italians had been devastated. Funnily enough, the Italian General Gelozo used to send gifts to his mistresses and charged them as «war costs»!

In Epirus, Macedonia and Thessaly, the Italians were the first to face the rising resistance movements, so their reactions were like those of Germans. In other words, they carried out harsh and disproportionate retaliation. For example, a concentration camp was maintained in Larissa until September 1943 where more than 1,000 hostages had been executed. Italians also approached the Greek Slavophones who lived in upper Macedonian territory near the borders. Thus, the Italian Pinerolo Division, which headquartered in Pindos mountain, recruited 1,000 of these Slavophones. The Italians frequently confiscated food from the villagers so as the Greek guerrillas could not get supplies from them.

Regarding the issue of nourishment of the Greek population, Italians were milder than Germans because they

2. The Triple Occupation of Greece

were aiming at permanent occupation of the areas. However, when the villagers supported rebel groups, the Italians troops did not hesitate to filch their villages before destroying them. Greeks mocked the Italian soldiers, who had succeeded in occupying Greece only after the assistance of the German troops. On several occasions, Germans also showed their contempt to Italians. When the Mussolini Fascist regime fell and Italy capitulated (on the 3rd of September 1943), Italian officers and soldiers in Greece took out their uniforms and wore ordinary clothes, in order to sell their uniforms as well as various materials and food to Greeks. Athens during those days had become a huge open bazaar. In fact, combat boots, weapons, bullets, motorcycles, musical instruments, blankets, medicines, and various tools were exchanged for gold pounds. The Italian army numbered 25,000 men while Germans were approximately 7,000 men. However, when Italy capitulated with the Allies in 1943, apart from only two divisions (Acqui and Pinerolo), the rest of Italian troops immediately surrendered to Germans.

Chapter 3

THE NATIONAL RESISTANCE
1941-1944

National Resistance Organizations

During the Nazi Occupation, several national resistance groups were formed. Most of them had nothing to do with the senior politicians who opposed guerrilla warfare and provocations. These politicians had the opinion that the retaliation of the occupying armies would not be proportional to the advantages of possible resistance. Many politicians were working to prevent the return of King George B', who had contributed to the Metaxas' dictatorship (1936-1941) and for this reason, was «persona non-grata» to them. A politician who supported the national resistance was P. Kanellopoulos (nephew of politician D. Gounaris, who was sentenced to death and executed after the defeat of 1922). However, apart from the political leaders of the big parties as well as the black-market traders and a few traitors, all other Greek citizens resisted the Nazi Occupation in their own way.

The main Resistance Organizations

The resistance organizationsDuring the occupation were many and began as early as 1941. The names and some characteristics of these organizations are described in brief:

-**EAM** (National Liberation Front), which was founded on the 27th of September 1941 on the initiative of the communist Party of Greece (KKE). It also integrated three other smaller left-wing parties. According to EAM's statute, the organization's objectives were: «...*to liberate our Nation from the present foreign occupiers and to acquire full independence to our country ...to form a provisional government of EAM immediately after the persecution of the foreign conquerors, which should have as its only scope the proclamation of elections for a constitutional assembly, with proportional representation, in order people express their views independently regarding the way they want to be governed. EAM also aims to consolidate this sovereign right of the Greek people to counteract every attempt that could impose solutions against their will and to eliminate any such attempt by all the means of EAM and clusters forming it*». In the second half of 1944, according to V. Bartziotas, EAM numbered 2,120,000 members. During the summer of 1942, EAM formed its military wing, the Greek People's Liberation Army (ELAS). Despite the fact that ELAS had previously arrested Colonel Sarafis and accused him of collaborating with the Italian troops, Sarafis ended up becoming the military leader of ELAS, along with his affiliates Andreas Tzimas (Political Commissar) and Athanasios Klaras (Chief Captain); the latter better known as Aris Velouchiotis was an agronomist and a hard-core communist, who had previously signed a «repentance statement» and had been disobedient to the leadership of the KKE. EAM-ELAS' administration were followers of the KKE, while the members of EAM and ELAS' guerrillas were not necessarily belonging to the KKE. The ultimate scope of EAM was to seize power through ELAS' forces and implement the «People's Democracy» (as misleadingly mentioned) or the «dictatorship of the proletariat» (according to the Marxist theory). This intention is generally confirmed by British officers, as well as by members of the KKE. EAM had also a subsidiary youth organization, EPON

3. The National Resistance 1941-1944

(United Panhellenic Organization of Youth), which integrated old OKNE (Young Communist League of Greece). EAM's mottos were: «National Liberation», «National Independence», «Republic, Not Monarchy», and «People's Democracy».

-**EDES** (National Republican Greek League) was founded on the 9th of September 1941 by an army colonel, Colonel Napoleon Zervas, who was a friend of General Plastiras (the leader of the revolution of 1922 after the defeat of Greece from Turkey).

The first statute of the organization proclaimed: «*...to fight using all forces and in every possible way, within and outside Greece, to strengthen the ongoing National Resistance, to contribute as much as possible in forming a National Revolutionary Army that would strive after victory to thrive for establishing a democratic, populist and socialistic form of government by voting on a referendum ...to appeal to the Allies: England, America, and Russia, as after the war the Greek citizens will be free to elect their government, avoiding the imposition of the monarchy. The decision of the Greek citizens obliges both political movements to accept it as final and to end the opposition to the state and the struggle. To prevent the returning of the King as well as his involvement in the free will of the Greek citizens... to aid in the representation of Greece, in the Peace Conference, by the elected representatives*».

It must be noted that Colonel Zervas was one of the rebels who were outlawed in 1935 and he strongly opposed the return of King George in Greece, but over the time he turned into a right-wing political leader, due to the rivalry between him and the communists. He mainly acted in Epirus.

-**EKKA** (National and Social Liberation) founded by Colonel Dimitrios Psarros, who was also one of the officers who were outlawed in 1935. The EKKA was mainly active initially in Macedonia and later in the mountain Giona. EKKA's armed wing was the 5/42 Regiment, which was kept far from both ELAS and EDES to avoid political controversy. The EKKA oath was as follows: «*I swear to keep faith in my homeland, to fight to death against the conqueror, to consider myself a brother to all the Greeks no matter which organization they support, as long as they are also fighting the conqueror*».

-**Eleftheria** (Freedom) founded in May 1941 by left-wing politicians in collaboration with the socialist Colonel D. Psarros.

-**Prometheus I and II** contributed to the establishment of EDES, but also managed the communication of many other organizations that did not have wireless apparatus, in order to exchange information with the British SOE in Cairo. Their leaders were originally Colonel Euripidis Bakirtzis and later Charalambos Koutsogiannopoulos, who was fond of EAM. His ability to communicate with the British in Cairo ended in February 1943, when he was arrested.

-**PEAN** (Panhellenic Union of Fighting Youths). Kostas Perrikos was the founder of the organization and one of the active members. Their mentor was the politician Panagiotis Kanellopoulos.

-**Bouboulina** organization was founded by Lela Karagianni (see later).

-**National Action**, was founded by P. Sifneos, Ch. Zalokostas, and Sp. Markezinis. Archbishop Chrysanthos was their mentor. The National Action had communications with the Middle East, organized the transferring of several Greek officers to Egypt, circulated unlawful publications as well as resistance newspapers and supported the return of the King.

-**YBE** (Defenders of Northern Greece) was founded on the 10th of July 1941 and most of its members were officers of the Greek Army.

-**PAO** (Panhellenic Liberation Organization) was formed by an evolution of the YBE group.

-**National Organization of Valtos**, which was a mountainous multipart entity northeast of Amfilochia in Arta and was founded by S. Houtas, who also worked in collaboration with EDES.

3. The National Resistance 1941-1944

-RAN (Romilia-Avlon-Islands) had as administrators the Chief General K. Ventiris and the Deputy General P. Spiliotopoulos. This organization collaborated with other resistance organizations opposing EAM. Beyond its military group, 1,200 students were included as members.

-Kodros had as Chief of Reservs, Navy Lieutenant Pan. Lycurezos, who was using wireless devices to send military information to the Middle East and contributed to the transportation of military officers to Egypt.

-Midas 614 was organized by the exiled government of Tsouderos. On the 31st of July 1942 Major I. Tsigante with his seven partners were sent in Peloponnese to coordinate the resistance organizations. However, Tsigantes and a few of his members were betrayed and killed by Italian Carabinieri.

-Yvoni was headed by I. Peltekis (code-named «Apollo») who would communicate with Cairo and undertook significant sabotage actions.

-Greek Patriotic Society (5-16-5) used to communicate wirelessly and sent information to the Middle East about enemy movements in Piraeus. Thanks to the organization's information, 55 vessels of the Nazis were destroyed. An important figure of its members, A. Kairis, was executed along with five members of his team.

-Fight-Anorthosis-Independence headed by Colonel Sarafis who would not be able to act independently because he soon joined ELAS almost compulsorily.

-Filiki Eteria of Evangelos Averoff-Tositsa, which was acting mainly against the separatist Vlachs.

-Omiros was a small group that was collaborating with «Kodros».

-Maleas and **Aliki** were headed by Captain E. Valasakis; the organization Aliki was sending officers to Cairo collaborating with Kodros.

-**Zeus**. It was a spy organization of Thessaloniki, co-operating with the British and its founder was the Police officer George Margetis

-**Athanasios Diakos** and **Odysseas Androutsos** were local KKE's organizations in Nigrita and Kilkis.

-**Democratis** and **National Solidarity** were KKE's organizations that soon merged with EAM.

-**Union Comrades of the National Struggle** headed by A. Fostiridis (his nick name was Anton Tsaous) in Drama and Thrace, which was fighting against the Bulgarians and later against ELAS.

-**Panhellenic Liberation League** was an alliance of ten National Resistance Organizations coordinated by lawyer P. Sifneos of «National Action».

-**People's Liberation Union** joined with other groups and formed the EDEM.

-**Single Democratic Liberation Front** was co-founded and supported by Sofoulis and Kafantaris.

-**National Association of University Schools** was a student organization.

-**Iera Taxiarchia** (Holy Brigade) was also a student's organization, which was printing and announcing notices.

-**Military Hierarchy** was an organization of Generals headed by A. Papagos; Five of the Generals were arrested and sent to Germany as prisoners of war until the end of the war.

-**Organization X** (pro-Monarchic and anti-communist organization) led by Lieutenant Colonel Grivas, who gave a strong anti-communist character to it; Organization X somewhat cooperated with the Middle East, to which they were sending out plans of the German forces, i.e., plans of the mines which were placed in ports; however, they avoided armed clashes with the occupation troops.

-**National Army** consisted of Non-communist groups in Peloponnese; it ventually merged with ELAS, while its members who did not agree with ELAS were executed.

3. The National Resistance 1941-1944

-**National Organization of Crete** led by Manolis Bandouvas; it was founded by the mayor of Chania N. Skoulas. He united all the non-communist resistance organizations of the island into the strong organization of **EOK**. The organization was not involved in controversy with ELAS of Crete.

-**National Hellenic Army** was made up of small resistance organizations mainly from Western Macedonia who were getting weapons from the Germans to collide with ELAS.

-**Independent chieftains**. There were many local leaders in northern Greece, mainly in Macedonia; in many areas, each village had a group of armed men with a leader, whose main mission was to protect the village against the arbitrariness of resistance organizations mainly ELAS

Organizational form and staffing of ELAS

The largest and most developed resistance organizations were EAM and its military arm ELAS. The communists had the command and administration of EAM. However, many non-communists had joined EAM because they did not initially know that apart from the resistance to the German conquerors, they had also parallel political goals. As far as the ELAS' administration is concerned, each military unit had three leaders: the Military leader, the Party leader of EAM (from the KKE) and the Captain (from the KKE).

The Greek guerrillas initially fought against the occupation forces, but in 1943 they initiated a civil war because EAM wanted to prevail over the other organizations and eventually integrate them. The military leader of ELAS, the Major General Sarafis initially had his own resistance group called «AAA». However, he was captured by ELAS guerrillas and after a strong psychological blackmail he accepted to join EAM and become its military leader. ELAS's captain was Aris Velouchiotis (Thanasis Klaras) who was a fanatic and a very ruthless man. Even KKE's Secretary G. Siantos disagreed with

Velouchiotis's actions. Andreas Tzimas, a communist lawyer and former MP, was the Political Commissar in the leadership of ELAS. Much sabotage took place during the triple occupation against the occupying forces. Some of the resistance organizations and their sabotage activities will be briefly described below.

The Bouboulina Organization

Lela Karagiannis, a mother of five children, organized a network with the main scope to help British as well as Greek soldiers and officers to go to Egypt. She also founded the illegal organization «Bouboulina» contributing to the resistance by sinking ships, bombing the airport of Tatoi and burning petrol as well ammunition stocks of the enemy. Moreover, she organized escapes of British prisoners from the Kokkinia camp. She was arrested twice by the German police (Gestapo). After her second arrest, she was tortured in the dungeon of Merlin Street and she was executed about a month later.

The sabotages of Ivanov

The swimming champion of Iraklis (Thessaloniki), Polish-born Jerzy Ivanov was an agronomist with exceptional studies who spoke six languages and was trained by the British in Lebanon and turned out to be an amazing saboteur with great action. He placed a clock bomb on a submarine that was then blasted by the explosion after departure from the port. He used the same method to blow up a smug Spanish ship and two ships in Patras that were carrying German ammunition. He also managed to blow up many planes at the airports of Hellenicon and Elefsina. He entered the factory of Maltsiniotis, where the Luftwaffe engines were repaired, and sabotaged them causing many defective airplane engines. He was collaborating with Lela

Karagiannis. Eventually, he was arrested by treason and was soon executed despite his attempt to escape.

Sabotage of the Organization Yvoni

The leader of the organization, I. Peltekis was organizationally ingenious. The main saboteur of the organization was Nikos Adam, who along with his colleagues placed magnetic bombs (turtles) at the hulls of the enemy ships that were in the port of Piraeus and blew them up. With such actions, «Yvoni» destroyed 58 vessels and 27 steam engines of the Nazi Forces. Yvoni also collaborated with Bouboulina's group. Yvoni was neutralized by Germans in March 1944. However, Peltekis managed to flee to Egypt; sadly, Nikos Adam and 52 other members of Yvoni were arrested and were executed.

The blasting of the ESPO building by PEAN

On the 20th of September 1942, an important sabotage action by the PEAN resistance group happened in Athens when the building of the National Socialist Patriotic Organization (ESPO) was exploded. ESPO was a pro-German organization and was tempting to militarily recruit Greeks on behalf of the multinational Waffen SS. Four heroes took part in the blasting: Captain Pilot Kostas Perrikos, the telecommunications technician Antonis Mytilineos, the law student Spyros Galatis and the teacher Ioulia Biba. The building blew up killing 29 Greek members of the ESPO and several Germans. The ESPO's leader Spyros Sterodimos was severely injured and died soon. ESPO after this sabotage was completely neutralized; sadly, the four saboteurs of PEAN were betrayed and arrested. Three of them were executed, except for Mytilineos who managed to escape. The traitor continued to betray the members of PEAN resulting in many arrests and executions; eventually, the traitor was discovered and was executed by PEAN.

Blasting of Gorgopotamos Bridge

The only great joint resistance action between ELAS and EDES was the blowing of the Gorgopotamos' bridge on the 25th of November 1942. The Head of the British saboteurs was Colonel Eddie Mayers and his main assistant was the Greek-speaking Captain Chris Woodhouse. Napoleon Zervas had the strategic direction of the operation and Aris Velouchiotis was present too. But the goal of the sabotage, with which Germans would not be able to have the facilities to transport supplies towards Africa, was obsolete; On the 23rd of October 1942 Rommel had been defeated in El Alamein and Germans were preparing to abandon Africa. Thus, the real value of that sabotage was negligible, yet the impact on the morale was great because it indicated that there was still hope for an overwhelmed Greek nation to resist against the conquerors.

Blasting bridge at Asopos river

British Colonel Eddie Mayers and Lieutenant Colonel Arthur Edmonds, with the help of specialized saboteurs such as Stott, Macintyre, and Wingate, decided after the success of Gorgopotamos to blow up the neighboring bridge of Asopos. Velouchiotis did not agree with their proposal, so the British acted alone on the night of the 20th of June 1943, blasting the bridge and escaping without losses.

The British Allied Mission to Pertouli

After the military landing in Italy in July of 1943, the British Allied Mission in Greece succeeded in having the major resistance organizations sign the agreement on the 26th of July

3. The National Resistance 1941-1944

1943. According to that the general leadership of all the resistance Groups would be left in British allied Missions and its headquarter would be in Pertouli, (where ELAS already had their Headquarters). At that time, ELAS comprised about 18,000 men, EDES 5,000 men, and EKKA 1,000 men. It was also agreed that «*all the National Resistance Organizations would only fight against the conquerors and not against each other*» as had happened before.

Battles and clashes of ELAS against enemy forces

ELAS guerrillas attacked various Italian and German squads resulting in many dead and wounded on both sides; however, the numbers of casualties announced by ELAS differ greatly from those reported by the occupying forces so there is no certain way for revealing the truth. In addition, according to the confrontation of Nazi Powers, ELAS also attacked the Greek gendarmes because they considered them traitors. Generally, ELAS' guerrillas used underhand tactics to avoid dealing with concerted enemy forces.

In autumn 1944, several leftist writers reported that more than 5,000 Germans were killed in battles with ELAS while fleeing from Greece. These numbers are obviously exaggerated since there were no so many serious battles that could justify the reported German casualties. ELAS was advancing towards the cities only after all Germans had already left.

The guerrilla attacks on individuals, Italian or Germans

ELAS used to attack separated individuals, Germans or Italians, but the conquerors reacted with horrible retaliation. Specifically, they used to burn the surrounding villages and kill the men, even the children. This tactic forced many villagers to flee to the mountains for safety. Perhaps such actions of the guerrillas were used as an indirect method to strengthen ELAS' number of men. Similarly, attacks on separated Germans were also done by EDES, but on a much smaller scale. An example of this sort of attacks is the case of the German physician Haas who was killed while his driver was injured after an ELAS attack guided by Captain Ypsilantis (A. Rosios) on the 24th of January 1944 on the road from Vatero to Xirolimni. The Germans in retaliation were outraged and blindly executed everyone in their way, 25 people in total; they also executed 42 prisoners. Doctor Haas was a particularly popular humanist in the region because he used to cure both Germans and Greeks for free. ELAS with a subsequent internal order recommended that «*all of our Units must refrain from similar actions*»; however, this was never the case.

Significant ELAS battles have taken place against 350 Italian soldiers in Oxinia. Also, ELAS attacked Germans on the street near Nestorio, in Larisa on the way towards Deskati, in Neuropolis airport, and in Amfilochia with many German deaths, and in Stimfalia against 200 German soldiers who attempted to steal a rural harvest. ELAS blew up a bridge near Karditsa and a train inside a tunnel in Kournovo that resulted in many deaths to Italian soldiers and Greek hostages as well.

Significant EDES battles and clashes with enemy forces

Zervas' rebels were mostly located in the mountains of Epirus. They contributed along with ELAS and the British to the blasting of the bridge at Gorgopotamos. EDES clashes were mostly done against the Italians. Significant battles of EDES took place under the «Operation Animals» in the straits of Macrinoros, in Neraida in Thessaly, in Agii Theodori and in Menina in the prefecture of Thesprotia. Since September 1943, many battles began against ELAS as well as against Tsams and Germans. Many Tsams had crossed the borders and went to Albania in order to avoid the jury due to their crimes. EDES' men finally were neutralized by the superior ELAS' forces, yet they were later reconstructed after the liberation of Greece.

Battles of the EKKA

Colonel Psarros and EKKA functioned for a short period and they were disbanded twice by ELAS on the 12th of May and on the 19th of June 1943. After the 31st of July 1943, the 5/42 Force successfully participated in some battles against the Germans. On the 17th of April 1944, the 5/42 Force was attacked by ELAS, Colonel Psarros was captured and executed after the order of Major Zoulas (despite that he was an ex-colleague of Psarros). Also, 62 men of EKKA were executed. All the men of EKKA that survived were incorporated in the Security Battalions to be safe.

Major civil conflicts between ELAS with EDES and EKKA

2/3/1943. Civil conflict: Arrest of Sarafis; the break-up of Kostopoulos' team and execution of Kostorizos who was a hero pilot of the war 1940-41.

18-19/3/1943. An Armed struggle with a guerrilla force of ELAS with EDES at the Tatarnas Bridge in Evritania.

07/5/1943. An armed struggle between ELAS' guerrilas and the guerrilla section of EDES in Trichonida by Dr. Georgios Papaioannou in Thermos, Aetoloakarnania.

13/5/1943. An armed confrontation between ELAS and EDES in Fthiotida.

13/5/1943. Capture and disbandment of EKKA by ELAS.

15/5/1943. An armed struggle between ELAS and the guerrilla Divisions of EDES Xiromerou.

29/5/1943. The second breakup of EKKA by ELAS; the cause was given by the autonomous actions of EKKA officers

Thymios Dedoussis and Georgios Kapetzonis, who were considered provocative to ELAS.

22-23/6/1943. An armed struggle between ELAS and EDES in Fthiotida.

1/7/1943. An armed struggle between ELAS and EDES in Filiates.

6/8/1943. An armed struggle between ELAS and EDES in Perivolia, Karditsa of Olympia.

5/9/1943. An armed struggle between ELAS and the guerrilla Division of EDES in Achaia, which dissolved.

8-9/9/1943. An armed struggle between ELAS and the guerrilla Division of EDES of Peloponnese on Mount Farmakas in Peloponnese, which later dissolved.

12-14/9/1943. ELAS's armed clashes with the remains of EDES of the Peloponnese, which dissolved.

3/10/1943. An armed struggle between ELAS and the guerrilla Division of the EDES Thessaly.

7-8/10/1943. An armed struggle between ELAS and EDES in Tsepelovo of Zagorohoria.

9-18/10/1943. The first round of civil conflict begins with EDES dissolution campaign by the Epirus Expeditionary Corps (ESI), led by Aris Velouchiotis; battles take place in many regions of Epirus.

31/10/1943. A Battle of Neraida; in this battle EDES is attacked by ELAS and the Tsams.

1/11/1943-29/2/1944. The civil war between EDES and ELAS is raging throughout the Epirus.

1-2/3/1944. Fight of EDES against ELAS and Bulgarians in Macedonia and Thrace at Agios Antonios of Kroussia and at the village of Isvoros.

26/3/1944. Fights between ELAS and EDES in Despotiko, Preveza.

27/3/1944. An armed confrontation between ELAS and EDES in Krania, Preveza.

3. The National Resistance 1941-1944

30/3/1944. Fights between ELAS and EDES in Krania, Preveza and at the same time battles between EDES and Germans in Thesprotiko.

10/4/1944. Fights between ELAS and EDES in Filiates at Kalamas River.

21/4/1944. Fights of ELAS and EDES in Florina of Valtos and Mesopotamos of Fanari, Preveza.

23-26/6/1944. An armed struggle between ELAS and EDES in Ano Rachi, Preveza.

29/6/1944. An armed struggle between ELAS and EDES in Glyki, Thesprotia.

18/7/1944. A battle between ELAS and EDES from Agiani to Meliki in Pieria.

21/7/1944. An armed strike of ELAS and EDES in Filiates.

1/8/1944. A battle of ELAS and EDES in Kalarrytes, Ioannina.

5/8/1944. A battle between ELAS and EDES in Kalarrytes, Ioannina.

7/8/1944. A battle between EDES and ELAS in Kalarrytes and Grammenohoria, Ioannina.

8/8/1944. An armed struggle between EDES and ELAS in the bridge of Kalamas and in Grammenohoria, Ioannina.

9/9/1944. Fights between EDES and ELAS in Anthochori, Metsovo and Keramitsa, Filiates.

10-11/9/1944. Fights between ELAS and EDES in the Kalamas Prelude in the areas of Northwest, Aghios Pantes, Aghios Nikolaos Filiates.

15/9/1944. Fights between ELAS and EDES in Macedonia; Bulgarian sections assisted ELAS and until the 4th of November EDES of Macedonia was dispersed.

15/9/1944. Fights between ELAS and EDES in Koukou and Sfandames, Pieria.

15-28/9/1944. Fights between ELAS and EDES in the city of Preveza as well as in Korfovouni or Brenissta and in Kourites, Filiates.

20-22/9/1944. Fights between EDES and ELAS, assisted by Bulgarian forces in Profitis Ilias and Koukos, Pieria.

18/10/1944 - 4/11/1944. A Battle at Kilkis, Macedonia, between ELAS and Anti-communists; EDES of Macedonia is dispersed.

18/12/1944. Armed clashes between EDES and ELAS in the villages of Bishduni and Botonosi.

19/12/1944. Fights between EDES and ELAS in Anthochori, Big and Small Peristeri in Ioannina.

21/12/1944. Fights between EDES and ELAS in Grammenohoria, Ioannina, in the areas of Grammeno, Kourenda, Soulopoulos, Bishduni, mount Driskos (Valaora, Prophet Elias).

22/12/1944. Fights between EDES and ELAS in the wider region of Ioannina, Arta, and Thesprotia.

23/12/1944. Fights between EDES and ELAS in Marmara of Ioannina, mountain Mitsikeli.

24-29/12/1944. Zervas transferred his men for their own safety to the island of Corfou.

The number of guerrillas fights that happend between EAM-ELAS and the other resistance groups or the state's, that occurred between 1943 and 1944 justifies the term «civil war» as well as the term «first round» used by many writers. These fights, as well as the Middle East coups (as it will be discussed later), greatly diminished the value of overall Greek National Resistance to their allies.

National Resistance in Macedonia and Thrace

There were many small resistance organizations in Macedonia and Thrace apart from EAM-ELAS, which were created soon after the occupation of Greece by the three occupying armies. These organizations sabotaged the enemy on several occasions and collaborated with the Middle East Greek

3. The National Resistance 1941-1944

government and the British agents. Specifically, they sent military information on the positions and movements of the occupying troops and facilitated the transfer of Greek military officers and soldiers to Egypt. The most important of these organizations was YBE (Defenders of Northern Greece), which was founded first in comparison with the others (on the 10th of July 1941) by Greek military officers and it was constructed in a military form. Later on, YBE was renamed as PAO (Panhellenic Liberation Organization). Nine out of ten of the officers in Macedonia had joined YBE/PAO willing to defend Greece's northern region, Macedonia and keep it within the Greek borders against the Bulgarian attempts to incorporate it.

YBE/PAO men cooperated with ELAS and armed villagers of Siatista in the Battle of Fardikambos against Italians on the 5th of March 1943. The battle was led by Colonel Kontonasios of YBE, and it was the greatest battle of the Greeks against the occupying forces. It resulted in 95 casualties from the opposing Italians along with 546 captives of war.

After March 1943, YBE/PAO and ELAS had many disputes because of the attacks by ELAS against the conquerors with no consideration of the retaliations that their actions would cause. At the same time, ELAS sought to assimilate or dissolve PAO. The officers of PAO I. Papapetrou and V. Avdelas were murdered by ELAS men. Chris Woodhouse offered to PAO to join with EDES in mount Vermio. However, ELAS reacted negatively and canceled the forthcoming agreement.

The leftists accused PAO of collaborating with the German army. A relative study of various texts reveals that PAO's guerrillas had roughly one-third clashes against Germans or Italians, one third against Bulgarians and one third against ELAS. Lieutenant Colonel Nicolas Hammond, who oversaw the British Military Mission, said that he had «... *excellent cooperation with YBE/PAO, which was run by career officers, and was very good at sending information to the Middle East Headquarters*». On the contrary, «*ELAS was too weak and inaccurate at collecting information about German intentions, although they had their own support system in the cities».*

PAO was set to be recognized as a National Resistance Organization in the Joint Allied Headquarters in Pertouli, on the 22nd of August 1943. But at the last moment, the Nomination Committee was influenced by ELAS that had objections. Their decision stated that «*the request will be reconsidered when PAO expels certain unpatriotic elements*». Colonel Mousterakis, who had represented PAO in Pertouli, «was detained for his own security there», until he accepted to join ELAS. During the last months of the Occupation, PAO officers evolved into an extreme anti-communist group due to the combined attacks of Greek and Bulgarian communists against them; ELAS, finally succeeded in breaking up PAO in 1944.

In the mountainous villages of Macedonia, local chieftains emerged and initially fought the Italians and the Bulgarians. However, they were harassed by ELAS and they were eventually forced to fight against both the Bulgarians and ELAS. It was now clear that ELAS was being controlled by the communist Internationalists.

Fights in Drama by Nationalists Pontians of A. Fostiridis

PAO collaborated with A. Fostiridis (Anton Tsaouss) who had a strong conflict against Bulgarians mainly in Drama (his nickname was Bulgaromachus (Bulagarian fighter) according to N. Hammond). Fostiridis had 250 men in his team, who followed him blindly to all of his guerrilla operations. In the Prefecture of Drama A. Fostiridis along with his men fought from 1943 onwards against Bulgarians, and later against ELAS. On the 5th of January 1944, Fostiridis's men surrounded ELAS Headquarters in Boz Dag, defeated them in battle and captured the British agent Miller (Guy Micklethwait), who was working till then with ELAS. Fostiridis assured Miller that he was

3. The National Resistance 1941-1944

trustworthy to the Middle East British and took him as coworker. In January 1944, Fostiridis was appointed as Head of the National Resistance Groups (EOA) in East Macedonia and Thrace, which numbered about 5,000 men and he had the general approval of the various chieftains and administration of the military officers, due to his capabilities in guerrilla warfare. His men were predominantly Turkish-speaking Pontian Greeks and caused serious damage to the Bulgarians. Fostiridis was very brave; he even attempted and succeeded in reaching the Bulgarian territory for collection of supplies even though he was attacked by Bulgarian guards.

The most significant success of the EOA against the Bulgarians was achieved in May 1944 at the Nestos Bridge near the village of Papades, where 160 armed Greeks confronted Bulgarians from the opposite bank; the battle lasted for three days. Due to the advantageous positions of the Greeks, the Bulgarians had many casualties (about 150 dead and wounded), while the Greeks had only 9 dead and 28 wounded. However, the EOA men were forced to leave because of the participation of the planes in the battle. In return, Bulgarians retaliated by attacking villages east of the Nestos River, where many homes were burned, and mass executions of civilians took place.

Rebels began getting supplies with German weapons

In 1943 there were chieftains who were opposed to communism in almost every village in Greek Macedonia. The Pontian Greeks were particularly fanatics as they previously had conflicts with the Bolsheviks of Russia. They were also experienced because they had fought in the Pontus guerrilla warfare. Even though they were speaking Turkish, they had a strong national Greek conscience. Following the break-up of

PAO in West Macedonia, many of the local leaders who defended their villages from ELAS attacks, started taking supplies from Germans who were thrilled with a civil conflict among Greeks allowing them to be calmer, even having limited military forces. The Gendarme's Commander K. Mitsou, assisted by the Sub-Commander Tzamaloukas, went to the mountain Kroussia as a team of YBE/PAO and had many clashes against Bulgarians. These two leaders repeatedly defeated and repelled the Bulgarians, who moved west to the boundaries of areas under their control (in the banks of river Strymon). After their opposition, the Bulgarians ceased to come west of the Strymon River and the Greek peasants were satisfied. On the 10th of December 1943, Mitsou did not accept the help with ammunition given by the Germans. On the 9th of January 1944, ELAS attacked the Mitsou's and Tzamaloukas' groups resulting in many casualties. The great lack of ammunition forced Mitsou to dismantle his team and flee to Epirus where he was incorporated into EDES.

In Macedonia, there were several men under the name of the National Hellenic Army (EES). A total of 5,533 men, fully supplied by Germans, were recorded. Their groups were mainly staffed by members of the Turkish speaking Pontian community, headed by three leaders, all of them named «Papadopoulos», one in each Prefecture: their Christian name were Michael (Mihalagas) in Kozani, Kyriakos (Kissa Batzak) in Pieria district and Konstantinos in Kilkis. The EES men were reinforced with weapons by Germans to face ELAS raids either in their villages or directly against them. At some point, the armed Anti-communists seized power and began acting at the expense of the residents who were fond of EAM. After the withdrawal of Germans from Greece, non-left guerrillas who were not arrested, despite the fact that they collaborated with the Germans, fanatically opposed the KKE. Those who were not convicted and survived the killing by ELAS' men, continued to fight against the communists until the end of the civil war in 1949.

The National Resistance in Peloponnese

In Peloponnese, besides EAM-ELAS, several non-communist-oriented resistance groups were also deployed to assist with the transportation of British troops to Egypt. A lot of small resistance groups were fighting along with British troops. The «National Groups Organization» and the «Greek Army» were organizations staffed by officers. They did not participate in any resistance actions of great importance in Peloponnese committed by the guerrillas, neither in the National Groups Organization, nor of ELAS, except for the Battle of Kerpini. (See below). The members of EAM-ELAS had created a vast network operated by their own people in the mountainous Peloponnese and they were taxed residents. They also were taking residents' food supply in order to feed the guerrillas. They established their own public and guerrilla courts and did not allow villagers to move from their villages to the cities because ELAS wanted to make sure that the villagers wouldn't betray their guerrillas' positions. The resistance organizations of the Greek officers wasted several months on organizational issues. They were disadvantaged by the fact that they did not have a supportive political organization. They had to ask for weapons from the British liaisons to fight Germans, yet they were most likely to face ELAS' hostility. The National Groups Organization facilitated Major Tsigante (Organization MIDAS) and assisted to his transportation to Attica by sea. Since they did not want to be incorporated into ELAS, they were targeted and attacked by EAM-ELAS. About 160 ELAS' guerrillas moved from Central Greece to Peloponnese to strengthen ELAS there. EAM-ELAS released a declaration calling all guerrilla organizations to incorporate into EAM, otherwise, they would be considered «rebellious against ELAS» and would suffer the consequences. The British were initially supporting ELAS mainly with weapon and supply drops, as it was the largest resistance organization, sprawling all over Greece.

On the 29th of August 1943, with the contribution of Major Harrington, the «Dyrachion Pact» was signed between the Greek Army and ELAS, aiming to the cooperation of the two organizations with Colonel General Giannakopoulos as the leader. This however actually meant the subordination of the National Groups Organization to ELAS. After a short period of hypocritical consensus, ELAS launched an attack on the National Groups Organization (from August to early November 1943), where several officers such as Major Karachalios and Lt. Vrettakos were killed. Colonel Papadogononas and Major Stoupas had since collaborated with the Security Battalions (SBs). Some officers accepted to join ELAS, while others were either hiding in Athens like Giannakopoulos, or escaped to Egypt.

EDES had minimum action in Peloponnese, but in September 1943 it was disbanded by ELAS and subsequently many non-communist military officers were executed. In Peloponnese there many atrocities were committed for political and personal reasons by both sides. Nevertheless, ELAS's behavior towards prisoners was appalling; Kosmas Antonopoulos reported 38 cases of group killings committed by ELAS groups, each of which killed more than five people who did not belong to EAM. In some of them, the victims were hundreds as in Meligalas and Feneos. After 1942, ELAS had organized 15 detainment camps where the non-communist were kept as they were considered the «opposition to EAM-ELAS». In these concentration camps, apart from the confinement and humiliations, a lot of executions also took place. Two prominent members of the KKE of Achaia were de-registered from the party because they showed unacceptable cruelty, and two others were jailed by a jury's decision because they made unjustified executions of citizens.

3. The National Resistance 1941-1944

An act of resistance was also the destruction of the Neda River Bridge on the 10th of October 1943, by British saboteurs and men of the organization «Greek Army», resulted in the destruction of all wagons of a commercial train.

Peloponnese suffered a lot from the retaliation of Germans in the resistance actions committed by ELAS, with the most dreadful one of Kalavryta. On the 7th of December 1943, ELAS members executed at Kalavryta 86 German prisoners. The victims were those that they had arrested during the battle of Kerpini on the 16th of October 1943. In retaliation, Germans killed about 870 inhabitants of Kalavryta's region. Following this fact, ELAS was not involved in any serious battles with the Germans but continued the clashes with the nationalist rebel groups, gendarmes and SBs.

National Resistance in Crete

The day after the Germans conquered Crete, on the 2nd of June 1941, 25 men aged 18-50 years old were executed by Germans in the village of Kontomari as retaliation from the civilian attacks against them. Various resistance groups were established in Crete following the German rule. Some of them were the following: National Committee of Crete which was formed with a model-based to the National Organization of Crete, the Pancretan Front of Liberation which was an organization similar to EAM, the Cretan National Revolutionary Committee, the National Liber-ation Organization, and others. In early June 1941, the inhabitants of the village of Kandanos opened fire against the Germans, killing 25 soldiers. On the 3rd of June, Kandanos was the first village in Europe which was completely burned by the Germans; they also executed 180 inhabitants and banned the survivors to return to the ruins of their homes. On the 12th of September 1943, guerrillas attacked a German military force near the village of Kato Symi; the German casualties from the battle were 70 soldiers dead and more than 40 injured. As revenge, the Germans destroyed all the villages of Viannos district from the Mirtos River to Amirus and executed 451 people on the 16th of September; they also destroyed 980 houses in 10 villages.

In addition to scattered attacks on Germans, two sabotages were carried out in Crete, at the airport of Kasteli, which was a base of German airforce: the first on the 7th of June 1942 and the second on the 4th-5th of July 1943, when many German planes were destroyed. The operation was planned by British agents under the name «Operation Albumen» and it was headed by the Danish Lieutenant Anders Lassen. The German Commander of Crete, Bruno Brieir, ordered in return the execution of 50 Cretans as retaliation. Moreover, in retaliation for Damastas' sabotage and for the attack on the German military base in the area of Anogia, Germans destroyed Anogia and later the village of Damasta. Another massacre due to the retaliation of the Germans took place on the 22nd of August 1944 to the villages of Gerakari, Ano Meros, Vrysses, Gourgouthi, Smiles, Drigies, Kardaki, and Krya Vrissi, where 164 civilians were executed. On the other hand, a blatant resistance act that took place in Crete was the kidnapping of General Kraepe in April 1944, executed by the Irish Major Patrick Lee Fermor, the English Captain Stanley Mosh, and several Cretan rebels. The British agents along with several other rebels managed to escape along with Kraepe in Egypt, 20 days later.

In general, Crete paid a high price for its fight during the invasion as well as the subsequent resistance against the Germans. Thanks to the Therisos' Agreement in July 1943, the civil war among Cretan resistance groups was prevented in Crete and there were no civil conflicts. However, especially in 1944, there were several attacks of ELAS on the gendarmes. It should be noted that the gendarmes participated in the Battle of Crete against the Germans and that many gendarmes were either

3. The National Resistance 1941-1944

imprisoned or executed by Germans because of their participation in the war and in the National Resistance.

The crimes of Germans, Italians, and Bulgarians during Greek Occupation

A plethora of crimes were committed by the German during the Occupation, including the circulation of unregulated foreign currencies, the forced loan, the appropriation of the agricultural production for their own needs, several thefts of the archaeological treasures, the effort to get Greek workers for the martial industries in Germany and Waffen SS, the ransom from Jews, and many more. It was typical that for the death of one soldier they usually executed 10-50 civilians while for the death of an officer they would execute 100 people; however, there were exaggerations even to this rule!

Table 2
A brief list of retaliatory executions by the conquerors
(except for the persecution of Jews listed in a separate chapter).
Usually the burning of villages would follow. The SS murdered even pregnant women, as well as babies, children and elderly people.

Season	Executed	Region
Jun. 1941	42 people	Alikianos, Chania
Jun. 1941	25 people	Kontomari, Chania
Jun. 1941	180 people	Kandanos, Selinou
Aug. 1941	44 people	Sines, Chania
Jun. 1941	42 people	Alikianos, Chania
Sept. 1941	~1,500 people	Prefecture of Drama
Sept. 1941	147 people	Choristi, Drama
Sept. 1941	238 people	Doxato, Drama
Oct. 1941	222 people	North and South Kerdylia
Oct. 1941	142 people	Mesovouno, Kozani
Oct. 1942	120 people	Prosilio, Fokidas
Nov. 1942	16 people	Ypati

Feb. 1943	117 people	Domenico
Mar. 1943	26 people	Camp P. Melas Thessaloniki
Mar. 1943	27 people	Farsala
Mar. 1943	54 people	Tsaritsani, Larissa
Jun. 1943	106 prisoners	Larissa
Jul. 1943	152 people	Mousiotissa, Epirus
Jul. 1943	20 people	Heraklion
Jul. 1943	10 people	Rethymnon
Jul. 1943	20 people	Chania
Aug. 1943	317 people	Kommeno, Arta *
Aug. 1943	49 Officials	Paramythia
Sept. 1943	84 people	Ligiades, Epirus **
Sept. 1943	13 people	Pefkos, Heraklion
Sept. 1943	49 people	Myrtos, Lasithi
Sept. 1943	114 people	Amiras, Heraklion
Sept. 1943	44 people	Eleftherion
Sept. 1943	451 people	Viannou, Lasithi
Oct. 1943	17 people	Eptalofos, Fokida
Oct. 1943	11 people	Lilea, Fokida
Nov. 1943	50 people	Argos
Nov. 1943	118 people	Monodendri, Laconia
Dec. 1943	696 people	Kalavrita
Dec. 1943	50 people	Patras
Dec. 1943	118 people	Draceia, Agria
Dec. 1943	50 prisoners	Tripoli
Dec. 1943	40 hostages	Prison of Gythion
Dec. 1943	119 people	Prefecture of Laconia
Jan. 1944	30 people	Patras
Jan. 1944	12 people	Camp P. Melas, Thessaloniki
Jan. 1944	30 people	Patras
Jan. 1944	456 hostages	Prison of Tripoli
Feb. 1944	40 people	Katerini Pieria
Feb. 1944	204 prisoners	Megalopoli
Mar. 1944	65 hostages	Karanona
Mar. 1944	50 people	Monodendri, Laconia
Oct. 1943	17 people	Eptalofos, Fokida
Apr. 1944	244 people	Sparta

3. The National Resistance 1941-1944

Date	Count	Location
Apr. 1944	280 people	Klisoura, Kastoria
Apr. 1944	318 people	Katranitsa, Pyrgoi
Apr. 1944	150 people	Lamia
Apr. 1944	64 people	Larissa
Apr. 1944	50 people	Kessariani
Apr. 1944	50 people	Veria
Apr. 1944	50 people	Corinth
Apr. 1944	6 people	Lamia
Apr. 1944	120 people	Agrinio
Apr. 1944	150 people	Metsovo
Apr. 1944	134 prisoners	Karakolithos
May 1944	200 people	Kessariani
May 1944	57 people	Prison Chatzikosta
May 1944	18 people	Camp of Chaidari
May 1944	16 civil servants	Athens
May 1944	46 people	Chalkida
May 1944	92 people	Kessariani
May 1944	100 people	Viotia
May 1944	24 prisoners	Camp of Larissa
May 1944	120 people	Camp of Chaidari
May 1944	86 people	Argolida Lake
May 1944	15 people	Vathotopi, Corinth
May 1944	40 people	Farsala forest
May 1944	22 people	Kometopi, Crete
May 1944	101 people	Camp P. Melas, Thessaloniki
Jun. 1944	40 people	Ag.Dimitrios, Zoupena
Jun. 1944	228 people	Distomo
Jun. 1944	67 people	around Distomo***
Jun. 1944	202 people	Kenouria, and Parnonas
Jun. 1944	28 people	Ypati
Jul. 1944	77 people	Skamnaki, Gythion
Jul. 1944	50 people	Sfagia, Thessaloniki
Jul. 1944	200 people	Liosia, Attica
Jul. 1944	50 hostages	Camp of Haidari
Jul. 1944	161 people	North Pindos
Jul. 1944	59 people	Kalyvia, Agrinion
Aug. 1944	61 people	Malathiro, Chania

Aug. 1944	164 people	Anogia
Aug. 1944	50 people	Mandra
Aug. 1944	15 people	block of Kalamaria
Aug. 1944	30 people	Damasta
Aug. 1944	9 people	Tymfristos
Sept. 1944	8 people (Jews)	Thessaloniki
Sept. 1944	49 people	Paramythia
Sept. 1944	149 people****	Chortiatis

* 97 of the victims were children; 74 of them were under 10 years of age
** they set fire and burned them alive and 40 of them were children under 10 years of age
*** among hese were 51 children.

The genocide of Jews and the Holocaust

The Jews of Greece suffered the so-called «final solution» (Endlosung) that was a monstrous program of genocide by which a total of six million people were murdered, directly or indirectly! The program for the genocide of Greek Jews was designed in Nazi centers of Berlin, Vienna, and Auschwitz. The German Occupation Forces in Greece and the Greek government did not have any participation in the study of this genocide plan. The «final solution» included:
1. Recording of Jews and their restriction to special areas (ghettos),
2. Setting of the David's star stuck on their clothes,
3. Transportation of Jews to concentration camps,
4. Selection of the capable Jews to work,
5. Execution with poisonous gas to those who were incompetent for work,
6. Extermination of healthy Jews by starvation and excessive work under hard conditions.

Most of the Greek Jews were living in Thessaloniki a big harbor of Greece's northern region, Macedonia. They had come to Thessaloniki after their expulsion from Spain in 1442. They

3. The National Resistance 1941-1944

were Sephardim and spoke Lantino (a Spanish idiom of Spanish Jews). The two richest people of Thessaloniki at those years were the Jews bankers Modiano and Alatini. Moreover, many Jews were scientists, traders, professionals, gold merchants, lenders; however, there were also very poor Jews that worked as transporters at the port. During the interwar period, the international anti-Semitism had affected many people in Thessaloniki.

Greek-Jews preferred to stand out as a local minority. In 1926 Greek-Jews participated in the national election under a «Jews political union». In a reaction against this, an anti-Jew Greek Party was established under the name «National Union HELLAS», with the acronym EEE or 3E.[2]

During the first year of German Occupation, many Jews were arrested and persecuted as communists, and many Jewish homes were confiscated and taken by Germans for their use. Hebrew newspapers and Jewish clubs were also forbidden. On the 11th of July 1942, the German Administration ordered all male Jews aged 18-45 years old to gather at Freedom Square of Thessaloniki, where they forced them to stand under the hot sun without water and without wearing hats for many hours. The Germans registered them and based on this list Jews were later sent to build roads and airports for construction projects. In October 7,000 Jewish workers were released, as their community paid to Germans a ransom of 2.5 billion drachmas; however, its only benefit was the delay of their displacement until next March. This payment was literally a robbery; Germans robbed an occupied country behaving like a «criminal gang»! In December 1942, Germans destroyed the old Hebrew cemetery of Thessaloniki where there were simple graves as well as artworks (sculptures). This cemetery was on the area of the current University campus. In February 1943,

---

[2] The 3E members were responsible for the burning of a part of Jewish' settlement, that was named Kambel in 1931. Prime Minister J. Metaxas abolished the function of 3E party.

the Reich Security Service began preparations for the displacement of the Jews. This operation was headed by Dieter Wisliceny, and Alois Brunner; both of them were close associates of the notorious Colonel Eichmann, who was Senior in the administration of implementing the extermination of the Jews. At that time, all Jews were forced to wear the yellow star and they were forced to live within the limits of their new region, the two ghettos. In March 1943, hundreds of Jews from these ghettos were sent to Auschwitz (in occupied Poland), in overcrowded and closed night train wagons. The place that they were sent was a camp that was used by the Germans as a «human death industry».

There were 77,377 Greek citizens of the Jewish religion in Greece during the time of the German Occupation; 69,151 of them were transferred to concentration camps, while 6,576 out of the 8,226 people who were not arrested, were helped by Greek families and were rescued. Around 1,000 others were able to escape in Middle East, while only 623 went to the mountains and joined the guerilla forces. A total of 46,091 people from Thessaloniki were directed to Auschwitz; only 1,950 impoverished people returned from there, all of them with horrific memories and a personal number was imprinted as an indelible tattoo on their wrist. Jewish missions to death camps ended in the summer of 1944 with about 59,000 people murdered there; they comprised 86% of Greek Jews, Romas, gays, several religious minorities, dissidents and mental sufferers.

The overall progressive deterioration in the living conditions of the Jews was apparent during the Occupation period in Greece. Thus, some of them escaped to Turkey and the Middle East or they became rebels in the mountains joining the Greek National Resistance to save their lives. Certainly, there were elderly Jews who could not be able to follow the rebels. Moreover, many Jews consi-dered as traitors by their compatriots if they become mountain guerrillas, since they probably left their parents helpless in the cities.

3. The National Resistance 1941-1944

The main leader responsible for the operation against the Jews in Thessaloniki was Captain Max Merten, who was a legal and inter-provincial advisor to the German army. Merten was responsible for plundering the property of the Jews. He was the one who ordered the destruction of the Jewish cemetery, which had significant artistic and archaeological value. Many historians attribute much responsibility for the events of Thessaloniki's Jewish people to Chief Rabin Zvi Koretz who was educated in Germany. He either did not appreciate what was happening or he just deceived his compatriots with the assurances about their security (even one week before the start of the trains to the extermination campsOut of 77,377 Greek Jews at that period, only 10,225 people survived. Several Jews were saved with the help of their fellow citizens who offered shelter in their homes. Many bishops gave fake certificates of baptism to save them, while Athens Police Chief Officer A. Evert issued 1,200 fake IDs. Moreover, Italian Consul General Guello Zamboni supplied with fake citizenship certificates about 300 Jews of Thessaloniki, thus allowing them to resort to the Italian occupation zone in Athens. Archbishop Damaskinos sent a courageous letter of testimony to Germans; no other religious Leader had sent a similar letter to Germans. Herein, it is worth mentioning the way that Jews of Zakynthos were saved and were not sent to Auschwitz: when the Germans ordered the Mayor of Zakynthos to hand over all the names of Jews of the island, Bishop Chrysostomos handed to the Germans a letter with two names, his own and the Mayor's one. Hence, the Commander, who was Austrian, showed flexibility and understanding. Regarding Jews who were living in Athens, about 800 of them, were sent to Auschwitz. The Rabbi Elia Barzilai of Athens and Mordenkai of Volos escaped to the mountain and they were saved. Thus, there was no founded lists of names of Jews who lived in Athens.

In order to manage the Jews' properties, a Law titled 205 was established in 1943 «on the administration of the seized and abandoned Israeli belongings» in the region of the General Administration of Macedonia. Meanwhile, the Israeli Property Management Service (YDIP) was established as a State Authority. Thus, civil servants or retirees were designated as interlocutors that meant to preserve the fortunes of the Jews who would be expelled out of Greece. The proprietors registered all the properties and handed over their statements to YDIP. After the war, several laws passed to return the properties to their old owners. The OPAIE (the Organization for the Revival and Reconstruction of Israel's Hellenic Republic), in turn, according to a Degree of 29/3/1949, received the fortunes that were managed by YDIP; but most of the beneficiaries did not survive. Many Jewish properties that had no heirs were assigned to the Central Israel Council. In 2003, the Greek government declared the 27th of January as «the Day of Remembrance of Greek Jewish Witnesses and Heroes of the Holocaust».

Organizations and pro-German parties of collaborators

The tolerance of the Greek Occupied governments and the strength of the German conquerors enabled pro-German and pro-Christian Parties to be formed. Such Parties were the National Socialistic Party of Greece headed by G. Merkouris who was a former MP and Minister, the National Socialist Patriotic Organization (the Greek acronym was ESPO), and the National Forces of Greece. These Parties comprised several friends to Germans, some nationalists, and a lot of opportunists seeking personal gains. Many members of these parties had preferential treatment by the Germans, such as food or taken Jews' property, and therefore they were unpopular. After the liberation, the founders of these parties were convicted as collaborators.

3. The National Resistance 1941-1944

Security Battalions

The Security Battalions (SBs) were founded by a Law issued on the 18th of June 1943. They were essentially troops organized and equipped mainly by the Occupation government, having their primary objective to fight EAM-ELAS and the KKE, which would eventually seek to seize power with weapons after the end of the war. The SBs consisted of nine Evzones' Battalions organized by the Rallis' government and 22 self-organized Battalions. Many SBs men were wearing German uniforms, while in the initial Battalions the troops were wearing Greek old-style uniforms. In October of 1944 the SBs numbered about 22,000 men. Their General Captain was Walter Simana, a Chech SS-Chief General in Greece. In Peloponnese, the SBs were subordinated to the local command of Colonel D. Papadogonas. The concept of founding the SBs came from the Greek Generals T. Pangalos and S. Gonatas and the resourceful I. Voulpiotis, but it was implemented by the Greek Prime Minister I. Rallis. The Statesman Th. Sofoulis had possibly accepted the idea of their creation. The two Generals had the idea of forming the SBs from democratic military officers to prevent the return of King George B' to Greece. But Rallis, foreseeing the plans of the KKE, founded the SBs to confront ELAS. Many of their commanders were known from the 1933 and 1935 military movements. The SBs enrolled officers and men of national resistance groups who had previously disbanded following ELAS' attacks.

It is worth saying that the SBs were formed in the summer of 1943, while Germans were based in Greece for over two years. The first men who joined the SBs were against King according to Pangalos' and Gonatas' suggestions, but those who followed later had a varying political origin, however, they were not communists; some of them joined the SBs to be safe from ELAS, some of them to overall secure their survival, others to avenge EAM-ELAS who harmed them, some others due to their anti-communist ideology, some young people because they liked to wear uniforms and hence display strength, while some others did it just from pure adventurism. It is important to mention that the number of ELAS' victims in Peloponnese was innumerable and had throughout the years accrued a lot of hatred. There are hints confirming that the creation of the SBs was at least temporarily approved by some British Services. British censorship authorities had indeed banned the Greek Intelligence Service from broadcasting radio allegations regarding the SBs. On the 2nd of February 1943, Von Paulus and his army were captured by the Russians after the defeat at Stalingrad, and in March 1943, Rommel has abandoned Africa. In the spring of 1943, it was almost certain that Germany was close to the trajectory of defeat. Thus, there is a critical question that comes up: why during the time when the fate of the war was turning against Germany some Greeks were asking to be equipped by -Germans? The explanation is probably that ELAS was aggressive against non-communists in the country and the other national resistance groups were pressed to seek help from Germans; this was the only way for non-communists to find weapons in order to defend themselves. Germans at this point were considered temporarily arms suppliers for the opposition to the communists. The SBs also helped Germans to recruit workers for Germany and support Germans' operations against ELAS. Yet, many SBs men created various troubles, thefts, and even murders. These actions have made SBs to produce discomfort for the Greek people. After citizens' protests for their arbitrariness, some SBs men were sentenced to death from Germans. However, SBs exhibited intense action against ELAS in regions like Peloponnese and Attica, which made them somewhat friendly to the non-communists, because of the terrorism and the atrocities of ELAS that had preceded. Papandreou described a crowd yelled cheering during a SBs parade in Athens but obviously the SBs ultimately acted to benefit the conquerors, and hence their formation and operation are considered condemnable.

3. The National Resistance 1941-1944

The pro-German Vulpiotis, during an interview several years later, allegedly said regarding the SBs: «...indeed, there have been atrocities and even criminal acts. However, they have also been involved in murders of innocent civilians, as exactly did the other side (ELAS). Who can be opposed to the fact that with the SBs we rescued the 'bourgeois regime' and prevented Greece from ashes»?

Many historians consider the SBs Fascist formations; however, this is not truth as in Greece, there was no Fascist Party like in Italy. The SBs had simply anti-communistic ideology and action. With the Caserta Agreement, which preceded the liberation of Greece, the SBs on the request of EAM were characterized as enemy groups and the government of the National Unity of G. Papandreou decided to disarm them, and this decision was favoring the communists. Many of the SBs' men were surprised by the government's decision because they were convinced that they were desirable and useful to the State after the Liberation. Lastly, when ELAS in December 1944 attacked Athens, many of the SBs men fought against it and thus avoided their future persecution as collaborators of enemies.

National Association of Anti-communist Action in Thessaly

The Battalions of the «National Association of Anti-communist Action» were organized in Thessaly by the Germans, with the main purpose of defeating the KKE and ELAS. They committed various extortions, thefts, and murders of the communists. They kidnapped K. Vidalis —a journalist of the left newspaper Rizospastis— from the train while he was traveling and killed him. Many members of these SBs were sentenced to long prison terms after 1944.

The problems with Tsams

Tsams are probably descendants of the Ottoman Orthodox Christians of Epirus who have acquired Albanian national conscience. They were about 28% of the population of Thesprotia and they were majority or totality in 35 of the 129 villages in Thesprotia. They had long ago opposed Greeks and sought to separate the area of Thesprotia (called Tsamouria by the Tsams) from Greece and to integrate it into Albania. In May 1917, when the Italian troops occupied Thesprotia, Tsams volunteered to become a part of the Italian army.

Following the exchange of populations, Venizelos' government in 1923 decided to make generalized expropriations of land and properties to give land to landless people. Thus, the Tsams landowners, like many others throughout the country, lost some of their estates and then rivalry was created with the rest of Greeks, the locals of Epirus and especially the refugees. After the regime of the 4th of August, Metaxas constrained the Tsams to speak only Greek.

During the Italian invasion of 1940, Tsams helped the Italians soldiers and served the invaders as provincial road guides. During the Occupation of Greece, they numbered a population of 19,000. They collaborated with the occupying forces of the Italians and enforced persecution against the Greek population. In various villages, they have committed many atrocities, such as looting, thefts, murders, massacres, women's rapes, and house fires. Moreover, they hampered the function of Greek schools. In July 1942, Tsams formed the Albanian System of Command Policy with 14 Battalions and sought the extermination or removal of the Greek population of Thesprotia.

When Italy capitulated with the allies, Tsams joint the local army of Germans, and they formed a special military unit in Ioannina, which was wearing German uniforms and behaved with callousness to the Greek population. Moreover, ELAS had recruited about 500 Tsams who participated in its civil conflicts

3. The National Resistance 1941-1944

with EDES of Colonel Zervas. In February 1944, the joint operations of Tsams and Germans resulted in the burning of Greek houses, they established 100,000 refugees and the murder of 49 Greek municipal officers on the 29th of September 1943. After these events, EDES of Colonel Zervas stood firmly against them and achieved significant victories in the two battles of Menina in August and September 1944. When the Germans left, the Greeks in Thesprotia retaliated and committed violent acts, since they had been furious with what they had suffered before. Many Tsams and their families went to Albania to avoid being tried as criminals. They took with them their property and the flocks of their animals. Subsequently, ELAS' superiority against EDES was accompanied by the temporary return of 3,000 to 5,000 Tsams to Thesprotia.

In 1945, the Court for the «collaborators with enemies» at Ioannina pronounced judgment on 1,930 Tsams as war criminals in absentia, while many of them were sentenced to death. At the same time, the legal procedure for the abolition of their Greek citizenship was completed. The farm property of the Tsams was assigned by law to the landless people of the area. It is estimated that about 18,000 Tsams left Greece. Based on the census date of April 1951, only 123 Tsams remained in Thesprotia.

Table 3.
Crimes of Tsams during the Occupation of Greece
(source: Ch. Lambrou)

Murders	632
Disappearances - abducted hostages	428
Rapes	209
Kidnappings	31
Fired houses	2332
Destroy of villages	53

Thef of sheep and goat	37556
Thef of cattles	9285
Thef of horses, mules, donkeys	4148
Thef of poultries	30
Thef of beehives	742

The Prince's State of Vlachs

The Vlachs of Greece are a Vlachophone population with Greek consciousness, mostly bilingual, who were engaged in livestock farming, commerce, as well as in science. According to the scholar K. Nicolaidis, the Vlach language comprises 2,605 words of Latin origin, 3,460 words of Greek origin, 185 words of Slavic origin and 150 of Albanian origin from a total of 6,657 words. It then apears quite like the Italian and Romanian languages. This linguistic similarity had prompted Italy and Romania to exploit Vlachs in order to expand their sovereignty. The national consciousness of the Greek Vlachs, as well as overall the Balkan Vlachs, has always been Greek. Many of them fought during the Greek revolution of 1821, some of them served as party leaders, politicians, ministers, Prime Ministers, Generals, bankers, professors in Universities, and national benefactors.

In 1862 the teacher Apostolos Margaritis (Vlach in origin) went to Bucharest and managed to get abundantly funded by the Romanian government, so he was able to establish the first Romanian school in Kleisura. In 1877 he was appointed «General Manager of the Romanian schools of the Ottoman Empire». In 1880, the «Macedonian-Romanian Committee» was established in Bucharest. There were 24 Romanian schools that were operated in Macedonia, a secondary school at Krusovo and a high school at Monastery. In 1886 a Gymnasium was founded at Ioannina and in 1899 a

3. The National Resistance 1941-1944

Commercial School was established in Thessaloniki. In 1892 the Romanians founded two administration authorities, one in Ioannina and one in Monastery, as well as 25 Romanian churches. In the summer of 1913, Magiorescou and Venizelos exchanged letters with their concerns regarding the Romanian educational and ecclesiastical autonomy of Vlachs in Greece.

During the First World War, officers of the Italian Expeditionary Corps had the initiative to establish the «Principality of Pindus» in cooperation with Vlach lawyer Alkiviadis Diamantis, who had conquered the mountain town of Samarina. However, the Diamantis venture was not successful as only a small number of Vlachs followed him. Moreover, the Greek government strongly protested and hence the Italians and Diamantis moved away. Later, in 1939 there were 309 Romanian schools in Northern Greece versus 3,666 Greek ones. During the Metaxas' dictatorship, Diamandis and his followers were closely monitored as possible Italian agents. Diamandis and the more prominent ones of his associates were preventively arrested and sent to a Corinthian camp, but Diamantis escaped shortly before Italy attacked Greece. As it turned out, some of Diamantis's people served as guides to the Italian troops during the invasion of Greece.

In the autumn of 1941, Diamantis —with Italian support— founded a military body called «Legion» (5th Roman Legion). The Legion's soldiers did various abuses and terrorized the Greeks. Diamantis aimed at establishing the «Autonomous Principality of Pindus», in order to unite Principality with Italy after the end of the war. Moreover, troops from Vlach legionaries were formed in many cities as well as the capital of Thessaly (Larissa) and Western Macedonia; they were supported by Italians with money and the carabinieria. However, the project did not succeed: of the approximately 140,000 Vlachs of Thessaly, less than 1,000 men ultimately joined the Legion. It has to be noted that many educated Vlach-speaking Greeks opposed Diamantis, such as Evangelos Averoff-Tositsas from «Filiki Eteria», a resistance organization founded to counteract Diamantis' efforts. Evangelos Averoff and other prominent Vlachs sent letters to politicians and Prime Minister Tsolakoglou, who promptly responded by sending instructions to the local state authorities. He also appointed Sarantis as the Prefect of Trikala who was a Vlach and a former officer trained in the secret war. Furthermore, the «Roman 5th Legion» acted against both ELAS and the Royal Gendarmerie[3]. Finally, the Legion was dissolved and Diamantis flew to Romania.

---

[3] The Greek Gentamerie was called Royal Gentamerie.

3. The National Resistance 1941-1944

The Slavophones during the foreign Occupation

The Slav-Macedonian National Liberation Front (SNOF) was an entity established in November 1943 by the Slavophones of the KKE which labored for Macedonia's autonomy. Its Head, Naum Peios, was elected by the 28th Regiment of ELAS. British leader Captain Evans favored the separatist actions of Peios. In January 1944, Andreas Tzimas as representative of EAM-ELAS and the Bulgarian Commander Kalchev on behalf of the Bulgarian army signed in Karydies Edessa the following Agreement:
1. The provinces of Kilkis, Paionia, Almopia, Giannitsa, Edessa, Aridaia, Florina and Kastoria are assigned by EAM-ELAS as SNOF's area of activity.
2. SNOF has the right to extend its zone of actions to other Southern provinces by securing full dominance in them.
3. The Bulgarian occupation army of Macedonia will undertake the occupation of the urban centers of Macedonia after the withdrawal of Germans and their surrender to EAM's authorities.
4. It was decided between EAM and SNOF to jointly establish an autonomous Macedonian State of a Soviet-like organization, which will ask to remain under the protection of the communist Soviet Union (USSR).
5. An initiative to establish a framework for the International Division to support EAM-SNOF was agreed; it was assumed that the International Division will be established at Kaimaktsalan area by Bulgarian officers who should provide ammunition.
6. The Bulgarians should take care to cover up any potential nationalist element in the occupation authorities so that no nationalist movement would be developed.

Greek Slavophones who were not incorporated in SNOF joined ELAS. The rationale of the KKE when founding the SNOF was to give a concession to the Yugoslav communists and to include Slavophone Greeks as guerrilla of ELAS. EAM kept away the autonomists Slavophones but all the heads of the KKE did not act similarly. In April 1944 a Regional Conference of SNOF from Kastoria was convened by the KKE in Dendrohori, where SNOF's anti-Hellenic aims became apparent. These actions led to a separation of SNOF from the leadership of the KKE in May 1944, as Siantos considered at the time that such declarations (supporting Slavophones autonomy) were not in the interest of the Party. The commissar of ELAS Andreas Tzimas met Tempo, the Yugoslav head of the League of Tito, at the Greek-Serbian border and discussed the creation of a Common Balkan Headquarters. This agreement included the sentence «*on the liberation of the population who lived in Greek, Serbian and Bulgarian Macedonia, as the mainstay of their struggle against the conquerors*». Tzimas on the 25th of June agreed with Tempo and the Albanian spokesman Kotsi Tzotzi that «*Macedonians of Greek Macedonia would fight for equal rights*», but the two representatives of the northern neighbors of Greece declared separately to be in favor of «*Self-determination of Macedonians*». On the 2nd of August 1944, a reconciliation agreement between the Slavophone guerrillas and ELAS was decided by which SNOF was remaining as a political organization while its military Divisions would cooperate with ELAS. On the 8th of August, at a gathering of communists in Monastery (Bitola) with Yugoslav and Bulgarian members of SNOF, it was decided to announce the «Federative Republic of Macedonia» as a state of Yugoslavia. Siantos and the Political Office of the KKE, after several amalgamations, did not accept these agreements and decided to dissolve SNOF; some fanatic of SNOF's members who disagreed were neutralized in Kastoria. A «Macedonian» Battalion under the leadership of Gochev who did not obey the directives of ELAS' Administration escaped to Yugoslavia and continued the propaganda on the autonomy of (Greek) Macedonia. Tzimas, who had become a permanent representative of ELAS in the «People's Liberation

3. The National Resistance 1941-1944

Front of Yugoslavia», managed to meet Tito who halted him by telling «...*if the reaction against the KKE prevails in Greece, Macedonia must join Yugoslavia*». Tito's policy was apparent: it was the enhancement of national consciousness in South-Slavs as «Macedonians» and the ultimate incorporation of the Greek province of Macedonia into the «Federation Republic of Macedonia». A lot of «tools» would be recruited for this: speeches, radio-broadcasts, texts, books, school lessons, maps, statues, clubs as well as a lot of money. Tzimas did not retreat to the demands of the Yugoslav communists either from patriotism or because he understood that this would politically harm EAM and the KKE; however, his further actions are somewhat unclear. He eventually fell into disgrace of his central party mechanism and he was later reported as a psychopath.

On the 23rd of October 1944, Gochev stated to the 9th Division of ELAS: «*Let us create a full popular organization, the Macedonian Liberation Front, to continue and accomplish the goals of ILINDEN*». About 1.200 Slavs participated in the 9th Division of ELAS. Following the latest events, ELAS moved against Gochev, but the Central Committee of EAM at Kastoria prevented his elimination and facilitated the escape of SNOF supporters to Yugoslavia. After the liberation from German and Bulgarian occupation in October 1944, Slavophones of Greece joined mainly ELAS and fewer of them the National Army; later, former ELAS's Slavophones joined the army of the communist guerrillas on the 1946-1949 civil war, while some of them did so, after compulsory recruitment by the KKE guerrillas.

Conflicts of EAM against other Resistance Organizations

In December 1942, a Convention of the KKE was held in Athens, which resulted in three important decisions:
a. to eliminate or integrate all other ethnic resistance groups,
b. to penetrate the armed forces that were in the Middle East,

c. to harm the king and Greek exiled government who were in Cairo.

The four major national resistance groups, which with their military staff established competition to ELAS, were EDES, EKKA, YBE/ PAO and EAO (Anton Tsaous group). These groups, as well as all other small resistance groups not controlled by EAM, had decided to be neutralized by ELAS. Civil conflicts began in 1943 while the hostile Occupation was continuing. The Greek guerrillas (ELAS, EDES, EKKA, YBE/PAO, EAO and other groups) initially were participated in national resistance actions, but then they started conflicts amongst them because EAM-ELAS wanted to lead or even to incorporate all the others. Thus, ELAS attacked: a. EDES of colonel Napoleon Zervas, b. EKKA of Colonel Psarros, c. the Macedonian National Resistance Organizations (PAO and EAO), d. the National Resistance Organizations of Peloponnese; consequently, a civil war was established among the resistance organizations (this period was later called the «first round» of the civil war 1943-1949).

The UK reinforced the resistance groups with weapons and money, but especially ELAS because it was the largest resistance organization. They were giving each guerrilla a salary of a golden pound per month. The gold pounds were inside tins that were dropped with parachutes in the mountainous areas occupied by the guerrillas.

There is evidence that in the Middle East Allied Headquarters of SOE, some British officers were leftists and therefore supported ELAS more than other resistance groups. Among others British agents Major Klugmann and his partner Gawe Berges were communists and members of the British communist Party; they were taking orders from the 3rd Communist International (Comintern); Also, the British agent Roufus Shepard who fell with a parachute among ELAS men supported them, as well as Captain L. Evans, who was living among Slavophones and he was considered as leftist too. On the other hand, E. Mayers and C. Woodhouse as well as Major Egg (Nicholas Hammond, the well-known archaeologist of Macedonia) and Donald Stott, a great saboteur from New-Zealand, had perceived what EAM-ELAS was aiming to, and informed SOE in Cairo accordingly. Moreover, Hammond accused ELAS of pursuing a civil war. It has to be taken into account the belief that the UK used to its policy the method of «divide and reign»; thus, after the initial support of ELAS, UK later opposed it. This may be related to the fact that the left-wing sovereignty was not clear to EAM-ELAS in its early phase, and EAM-ELAS as the largest guerrilla organization in Greece had initially attracted the British admiration. Actually, there was a difference in policy between Churchill and the SOE in Cairo. The latter was supporting strongly ELAS (due to SOE's leftish agents as it was written before) but Prime Minister Churchill and Eden (minister of Exterior) supported the exiled Greek government and the return of King George B' to his throne.

The Donald Stott's initiative

Donald Stott came to Greece and undertook various sabotage operations to the enemy; one of them was done on the bridge of Asopos. In autumn 1943, Stott met the representatives of the National Action, the United Democratic Liberation Front, the Organization X, EDES of Athens, the National Organization of Crete, the PAN and the Triaina in Athens and signed an agreement under which they set up their organizations under the command of the Middle East Headquarters of SOE to carry out sabotage and espionage operations against Germans. They also agreed to protect and keep the order in the cities until the arrival of allied troops and to prevent the violent predominance of EAM-ELAS.

Through the Mayor of Athens Georgatos, a meeting with Stott and German officers took place on the 13th of November 1943, where a separate capitulation between Britain and

Germany was discussed. However, Stott had no authority for this initiative and thus, SOE called him back to Cairo.

The capitulation of Italy with the Allies

In September 1943, Italy surrendered and thus stopped fighting. The Italian Commander in Greece signed a Pact, according to which the Italian troops would be controlled by Germans. Only two divisions from all Italian military units did not surrender, Pinerolo Division in Thessaly and Acqui Division in Kefallinia. The Commander of the Acqui Division arrested 650 Germans and sent them as prisoners to southern Italy. In reprisal, Germans on the 11th of September bombed Corfu for 11 days causing mostly Greek victims. They also attacked the Acqui Division with no mercy; they had executed thousands of prisoners, while a lot of the survivor prisoners were loaded on a ship that sank by an explosion in sea, with many Italian losses. On the other hand, the Pinerolo Division decided to surrender to ELAS and fight the Germans; the agreement was signed by Generals Infante, Sarafis and Woodhouse.

ELAS soon disarmed the Italians, took their heavy weapons and ammunition, and hence they became a powerful army. ELAS claimed that EDES had agreed with the Germans not to attack them; however, this was false as it was revealed later by the British archives. ELAS' captain Fotis Vermeos (Phivos Grigoriadis) wrote: «... *to justify ELAS's attack on EDES, ELAS spread fake information that Zervas signed an agreement with Germans*». Also, Thomas Dritsas (Petros Argyropoulos) in his letter to the newspaper Avgi on the 4th of October 1981 pointed out: «... *beyond smirching our political opponents, we had no evidence that Zervas had agreed to cooperate with Germans in operations against ELAS in Epirus*». Moreover, N. Hammond has written: «...*in EDES region, cooperation with the Allied Military Mission and the Operational Greek Teams was good, while important operations against the German artillery in*

3. The National Resistance 1941-1944

Paramythia were successful, which however never happened in areas controlled by ELAS». In July 1944, Sarafis sent a message to the Middle East Allied Command complaining of lack of ammunition. However, it is known that ELAS avoided engaging in serious battles with Germans by retreating and changing positions, apparently to preserve ammunition and use them later against EDES. In July General Wilson sent a message to Sarafis saying: «*Any Greek who abuses or attacks a member of the Allied Mission or personnel under his direct supervision will be treated as a war criminal after the war*». Germans on the 16th of October 1943 attacked EDES forces in Epirus. Zervas was defending successfully his positions for 10 days, but five Battalions of the Mountain Brigade were added to the German forces. As Zervas was fighting back he found out that he was between two armies: the German army and ELAS fought EDES for four days and the subsequent fifth night (on the 30th of October), Zerva's men followed his instructions and they moved in safety unnoticed. The German army continued their operations by attacking groups of thieves, but also by burning villages; more than 200 villages were destroyed, among them Pertouli. ELAS was constantly retreating against the Germans and moving away from their forces avoiding a direct battle. ELAS co-operated closely with the Albanian communist party leader Emver Hotza, who neutralize the nationalist North Epirus Liberation Front (MABH) fighters.

Internally, the internationalist duty of the KKE-ELAS prevailed over the national one. In the spring and summer of 1943, ELAS was in a dilemma: should it participate in a joint Balkan Military Headquarters, along with Serbs, Albanians, and Greek Slavophones, or to join the Headquarters of the Middle East? Velouchiotis strongly supported the first case while Tzimas in a meeting he had with the Yugoslavs did not agree. According to Markos Vafiadis, G. Siantos chose the second option and canceled any agreement for not breaking up EAM due to the Macedonian issue. At that time, the British SOE were supplying

ELAS with ammunition and paid salaries to the guerrilla fighters, so any break down with them would not be advantageous! In September 1943, the First «Pan-Macedonian meeting of EAM» was held in Elafina (in Pieria) and it was decided a «*military combat against the conquerors and the autonomists*».

The agreement of Plaka and the efforts of the British agents for unity of the resistance groups

The winter of 1943-1944 was very heavy and the actions of all, ELAS, EDES, EKKA had been restricted as well as their inter-conflicts. The British Allied Mission with Hammond and Woodhouse in co-operation with American officer Wise, succeeded in signing on the 29th of February 1944 an agreement of the resistance Units (the Myrophylo-Plaka Agreement of Epirus), defining their areas of responsibility; it was a truce. Based on this, all teams would only fight against Germans. Aris Velouchiotis did not participate in the discussions by the decision of the leadership of the KKE, obviously because he would be opposed.

The Plaka agreement included the following: a. cessation of ELAS-EDES hostilities, b. conservation of the territories owned by them on the day of the agreement (ELAS, EDES, EKKA), c. launch of joint actions of the three organizations against the conqueror, d. the Joint Committee would oversee the implementation of the Agreement, e. release of detainees caught in previous conflicts, f. military help by the British SOE of all Resistance Organizations proportionally, g. condemnation of SBs and the government of Rallis as betrayers, h. the obligation of all Resistance Organizations to participate in the «Noah's Ark» Alliance Plan, according to which the exiled government would return from Cairo to Athens.

3. The National Resistance 1941-1944

The Plaka Agreement favored EDES, which had fewer soldiers than ELAS. EAM-ELAS accepted the terms of the agreement because otherwise the British would stop supplying them with sovereigns and guns (these were dropped to the mountains with parachutes); however, the truce of the two major opponents did not last long.

Meanwhile, British and American planes were bombing military targets and sometimes these bombings concerned city areas. On the 11th of January 1944, 80 female students of a school in Piraeus suffocated under ruins, after a bombing from allied air forces; there was no logic for this tragic incident, since Piraeus was not a military target as was e.g. Berlin. In June 1943 ELAS broke the 5/42 army constitution of Psarros. The following conversation of E. Mayers with A. Velouchiotis had been recorded after the dissolution of Psarros 5/42:

Magers: «This act of ELAS is hostile and is directed against the Middle East Allied Headquarters because the 5/42 Regimen is a coalition that was formed under its command».

Velouchiotis: «And ELAS is an ally of the Middle East Army».

Magers: «I agree but this is a hostile act and will greatly slow down the liberation of Greece».

Velouchiotis: «This is about us, please do not interfere with the internal affairs of the country».

Psarros: «What happened means the beginning of a civil war. It is a big political mistake and it will cost you a lot and will divide Greece again».

Psarros was an ideologist socialist, an old pro-Venizelos military officer of the 1935 movement and a pure patriot. He was an old close friend of Sarafis. The General Headquarters of ELAS, after Psarros' death, issued a statement saying that EKKA was cooperating with SBs, which did not happen until his death. The surviving men of Psarros eventually managed to arrive in Patras and despite their British uniforms, they were assigned to SBs for their security.

Woodhouse wrote in 1978 about Zervas: «...*I want to emphasize this and insist on this truth; Zervas has always been faithful to our alliance and has never done the slightest thing at the expense of the common struggle, nor anything to help the common enemy*».

Greek politicians and militaries in the Middle East

In March 1942, King George and the PM Tsouderos tried to reorganize the Greek army. Eventually, P. Kanellopoulos took over the Vice-Presidency of the government and the supervision of the War Ministry. But the officers and politicians who moved in Egypt did not cease to discuss politics and to conspire against their political opponents. The Democratic detachments of 1935 had returned to the army indiscriminately and put them against the King and Metaxa's military officers, but the latter had the glory as of defeating the Italians in the war. In addition to this rivalry as a continuation of the national division of 1915-1935, the KKE was a new parameter of the political «game» and its followers organized a coup against the exiled government.

The Middle Eastern Movement of March 1943

The rebel Movements in the Middle East were created because there was an infiltration of leftists in the Greek army. Organizations such as the Anti-Fascist Military Organization and the National Liberation League had transmitted the morals of EAM to many officers, sergeants, and soldiers. Competition between officers (ideological differences as well as the conflict for the seniority list that had been corrupted by dismissed officers) brought up controversy, lack of discipline as well as other issues. Three Movements were attempted on this substrate, with the last one being the largest. On the 17th of February 1943, the men of an infantry Battalion revolted, and the chaos was scattered to the entire 2nd Brigade as well as to the 1st Brigade. The officers who had resigned, plus 150 soldiers from the rebellious units, were arrested and detained at the Merz Ayum camp. The minister of Military Affairs P. Kanellopoulos was attacked by angry rebels who put his life in danger. On the 31st of March 1943, army officers in Egypt asked for the Prime Minister Tsouderos' resignation. Many officers were arrested by rebel soldiers. Kanellopoulos reacted by removing officers who favored the Metaxas regime, yet this was perceived by the rebels as governmental weakness and therefore they proceeded to the next Movements.

The army Movement of July 1943

In July 1943 revolts began in the Navy, and in particular between the warriors of the ships «Ierax» and «Miaoulis». At the same time, the 2nd Brigade revolted. There had been anti-disciplinary actions, pounding of officers and chaos that alarmed the Allies. Deaths penalties were assigned to the originators (finally, only two were executed) and the 2nd Brigade was disbanded with British intervention.

The army Movement of April 1944

On the 3rd of April 1944, the Movement was spread in all Greek army, navy and aviation Units. The British officers became anxious about the fleet's overall situation and deactivation because the Greek navy was very helpful in participating in convoys. Before long, all the Units of the warships were occupied by communist sailors, who propelled the officers, practiced violence, while some officers were even thrown into sea. Moreover, rebels were circulating on the streets and they seized their superiors in rank. At the military camps, the hierarchy had been abolished and the Units were commanded by committees of leftist and junior officers. These events were absurd for the army, which must function with discipline. On the 13th of April 1944, Emmanuel Tsouderos resigned and King George B' appointed Sophocles Venizelos as Prime Minister of the Exiled government. The new Prime Minister appointed Admiral P. Voulgaris for the position of as Naval Secretary, with whom within a few days they set up a group of Greek «commandos» that on the 22nd of April took over again the control of the ships after fierce battles, with victims on both sides. Hundreds of army and aviation soldiers had been arrested as rebels by British armed forces and they were restricted in camps. After twelve days, Venizelos, despite his successful dealing with the revolt of the leftist soldiers, was asked by the British administration to resign because the KKE would not accept him in the new government. With no delay, George Papandreou, who was Churchill's favorite, was appointed as Prime Minister and formed a «National Unity government» to clear the air.

Regarding the Middle East Movements, P. Kanellopoulos stated: «…This spirit of EAM had been transferred to the Middle East: as spirit of Civil War; as spirit of hatred; as spirit of derangement in the military hierarchy, which had been successfully implementing during the war in Epirus; as the spirit of humiliation of the superior by the inferiors; as rule of calumniation, cursing and bawdiness». These Movements disordered completely the Middle East army, which fell in disgrace and the Greek glory of 1940-1941 faded, while the Greek contribution to the allies' effort became unreliable! Only the 3rd Mountain Brigade and the Holy Lodge (comprised of officers) remained intact and reliable. The British authorities decided to imprison 8,000 protesters from a total of 18,500 men. Their leaders were sentenced to death by a Maritime Court, but their sentences were not executed. All the rebels were transferred to concentration camps in Sudan, where they stayed under very bad conditions.

3. The National Resistance 1941-1944

The Greek ships were activated again in June 1944 and helped the allied landing in Sicily, where they also transferred the 3rd Greek Mountain Brigade that fought bravely and entered Rimini first. Stalin was not involved in the Middle East Movements, which was logical since there was still a need to strike the Nazis. Moreover, there was probably no guidance by the Greek EAM to the movements in the Middle East. Apparently, there was an auto-nomous communistic movement organized locally in Egypt.

The government of the PEEA

On the 10th of March 1944, in Viniani of Evritania, a political government of EAM at free mountainous Greece was formed under the name of «Political Committee of National Liberation» (PEEA). Initially, General E. Bakirtzis was appointed as President of PEEA, while a month later he was replaced by A. Svolos, who was a Professor of Constitutional Studies and a socialist. The government of the mountain comprised of Ministers, among others, the socialist E. Tsirimokos (Justice), Prof. A. Aggelopoulos (Finance), Prof. P. Kokkalis (Social Welfare), General E. Mandakas (Military) and the KKE Secretary G. Siantos (Interior Affairs). On the 25th of March 1944, Stalin sent a congratulatory telegram to King George B', for the National day of Greece. This gesture showed that the USSR recognized the exiled government in Cairo and not PEEA. This event created embarrassment at the KKE and EAM who organized «elections» a month later by secret ballot. The elected persons voted after five days for the representatives of the so-called «National Council». People voted in secret in the non-occupied villages of the country as well as in Athens but obviously, many populations could not vote. The 184 delegates who were elected were fond of left-wing parties, while only a few of them were independent. Moreover, 22 members of the previous Greek Parliament remained in the National Council. In general, the fact that only leftist delegates were elected, illustrates that the one-party form of the USSR elections was implemented.

On the 27th of May 1944, the «Resolution of Koryschades» was finalized and approved by PEEA, which comprised a kind of a Constitution and included 15 fundamental articles. In summary, the resolution declared: *«all power is derived from the people»* but also *«exercised by the people»* and that *«independence and popular justice are fundamental institutions of the public life of the Greek people»* and *«popular freedoms are sacred and inviolable»*, proclaiming *«equality of civil rights for both men and women»*, while regarded labor as *«a basic social function that creates the right to enjoy all goods of life».* The Resolution also recognized ELAS as a National Army: *«ELAS is an armed faction of the Nation fighting for the liberation of the homeland and the freedom of people».* Eventually, PEEA broke down on the 5th of November 1944, as the KKE and EAM agreed to participate in the «National Unity government» under Prime Minister G. Papandreou. On the 26th of July 1944, the Russian Colonel Grigori Popov and seven men using a Russian aircraft were landed in the Neraida airport near the Headquarters of ELAS. The left persons of ELAS Headquarters were excited by the Soviet presence on the mountain; actually, Popov was acting as Stalin's «eyes and ears». He stayed on the mountain until the country's liberation and then moved to Athens, where he was in touch with Papandreou's government, yet without having substantial responsibilities. At the end of July 1944, a two-day meeting of the Central Committee of the KKE was held on the mountains, where G. Siantos instructed V. Bartziotas to prepare his men to take power in Athens and he said that all ELAS Divisions would move towards Athens.

3. The National Resistance 1941-1944

Departure of E. Mayers

Chief Brigadier E. Mayers, due to his apparent disagreement with the British Headquarters of SOE in Cairo, was ordered to go for talks to Cairo and then to London. Mayers informed his superiors that he convinced that EAM-ELAS would violently acquire government power at the first opportunity. He had such talks among others with the Prime Minister Winston Churchill. A similar update to the British Foreign Ministry was made by a letter from Major David Wallace who spoke Greek. Lieutenant Colonel Nicolas Hammond was the Head of the British agents in Greek mountains of Western Macedonia until August 1944, when Superior Brigadier Barker Benfield arrived in the country and took over as the new leader. Hammond was supporting PAO as a pure resistance organization, opposing ELAS' objections on this. The rivalry of ELAS with PAO was very intense and Hammond tried to persuade Siantos to accept PAO as a resistance organization. Finally, EAM-ELAS, EDES, and EKKA signed Plaka's Agreement without PAO, due to strong objections of ELAS. When ELAS conflicts resumed with EDES, the British officers notified the Middle East Authorities to stop supplying weapons to ELAS. Hammond later wrote in a book about ELAS that «...*its main activities (ELAS) were the civil war with EDES as well as later the cold war against it and then the destruction of EKKA (5/42 Constitution) ...Their main purpose was to destroy the operational Greeks who did not belong to EAM*». However, EAM and PEEA representatives stated: «...*the Resistance and bloody struggle of Greeks in the cities and on the mountains was in such form that the moral significance of the reckless actions of foolish people, despite stemming from the desire of national unity, led to demeaning and devastating effects and must be condemned by everyone....*».

The Lebanon Agreement – National Council

George Papandreou was a democratic socialist who at the beginning of the foreign Occupation published an illegal newspaper under the title «Eleftheria» (Freedom). For his activities was put in prison for three months. In 1944 Papandreou wrote an extensive memorandum and sent it to the British where he predicted post-war development; he wrote that *«the interests of Greece and the UK for the first time in history are common»*. Moreover, his analysis was interesting and predictive: *«... Nevertheless, a new form of global competition is emerging. Two world fronts are being shaped: the communist Pan-Slavism and the Liberal Anglo-Saxonism. ...these two trends will eventually meet, and their only difference will be on the great issue of freedom: individual, political, ethical»*.

Papandreou traveled by a small boat to Turkey and thereafter reached Cairo by airplane on the 14th of April 1944. His interesting memorandum, his ability to shape problems and the articulation of his speech attracted the interest of the British authorities in Cairo. Thus, he was appointed on the 26th of April 1944 as Prime Minister of the exiled government of Greece. Within 13 days he organized the Lebanon Conference under the full support and the auspices of the British. The Conference was held in a hotel in Dur-El-Sawer in Lebanon, where the delegates were isolated. Among others, the English Ambassador Reginald Leeper attended closely the discussions. There were also representatives from all Greek parties, among them from the KKE, EAM, ELAS, and PEEA. Papandreou criticized in his inaugural speech EAM-ELAS for their scopes and tactics. In the end, the delegates of EAM and of PEEA announced a joint condemning statement against the Navy Movement in Egypt. It should be noted that ELAS' attack on EKKA and the execution of Psarros and many of his men assassinations were very recent events and therefore the delegates from the KKE-EAM-ELAS were in a difficult position;

3. The National Resistance 1941-1944

perhaps, this made them accept the agreement that remarked on… *«destroying EAM's terrorism»*!

A passage from a Papandreou's speech which was given on the 17th of May 1944 is the following: *«...The responsibility of EAM is that it did not only aim at the resistance against the occupation forces, but wanted to be prepared for post-war dominance. For this, it sought first the monopoly of the National struggle. It prohibited anyone else to go to the mountains for fighting the conqueror; only ELAS was permitted. Greeks were prohibited to act their national duty under the danger of death penalty. An old paradigm is that of Colonel Sarafis and a recent one that of the absent Colonel Psarros; EAM attempted the horror and terrorism of their opponents....The rivals of EAM were considered enemies of the homeland. ...Thus, a vicious circle has emerged to which our people are suffering. Guerrillas, National Organizations and Security Battalions are counteracting. This is the vicious cycle that we ought to end soon. And there is only one way to do so. The elimination of the class-Army and the establishment of a National Army...»*. After long talks lasting three days, an Agreement was reached on the 20th of May 1944, which was called the «National Contract» and it was signed by all the participants of the «Lebanon Conference». The Agreement was composed of the following main chapters:

«1. Condemnation of the rebel Movement, the punishment of the instigators, re-ordination, and control of the armed Greek Forces in the Middle East under the flag of the Greek homeland;

2. The unification and control to the orders of the National Union and the Allied Headquarters of all the guerrillas of free Greece, as well as the recruitment, when time comes, of all the combatant forces of the nation against the conquerors;

3. The abolition of EAM's terrorism in the Greek countryside and the consolidation of the personal security and political liberty of people on the conqueror's withdrawal;

4. The continuous care for the adequate supply of food and medicines in enslaved Greece, as well as the mountainous homeland;
5. The safeguard of the forthcoming liberation of the country, the order and the freedom of the Greek people to liberate themselves from physical and psychological violence, and let them decide in principle of both the type of governance and their social system too;
6. The imposition of tough sanctions against the traitors and the exploiters of the despair of the Greek people;
7. The provision for immediate fulfillment after the liberation of the needs of the Greek people;
8. The fulfillment of our National Rights; our vast services and sacrifices, the holocaust that happened in our country cannot have any reimbursement other than the establishment of a new and free Greece».

When EAM-ELAS' leaders on the mountains learned about the Lebanon Agreement, they were very upset, and they decided to withdraw their delegation. Sarafis returned first and spoke with Ioannidis for his reservations. Siantos was very angry, and Zevgos was also angry and he tried to disengage their lazy representatives, Roussos, and M. Porphyrogenis at the Lebanese Conference.

The Russian Colonel Popov advised EAM to accept the Lebanon Agreement and to employ their Ministers in the government of National Unity under Papandreou. Ultimately, the only thing that happened in EAM headcourters was to criticize Roussos and Porphyrogenis for their policy in the Lebanon Agreement.

The Caserta Agreement

In mid-June 1943, the British Colonel E. Mayers asked Sarafis and Zervas to amplify their attacks to Germans so that they would believe that the Navy of the Allies' landing was impending

3. The National Resistance 1941-1944

in Greece and not in Italy as it was aimed initially. Thus, ELAS and EDES began harassing the Germans. On the 21st of August 1944, Papandreou discussed with Churchill in Rome the possibility of sending British troops to Greece. On the 31st of August, Minister of Foreign Affairs F. Dragoumis complained that the ceasefire agreement with Bulgaria did not include compensation for Greece. The Bulgarian government immediately declared war against Germany but didn't participate in any millitary action. This change helped Bulgarians to cooperate closely with ELAS, but it is also responsible for the very mild treatment of Bulgaria by the Allies in the peace conditions. On the 26th of September of 1944, in the city of Caserta, South Italy, an Agreement was signed between the «free Greek government of National Unity» (with delegate G. Papandreou) and the resistance organizations of EAM (with delegate S. Sarafis) and EDES (with delegate N. Zervas), to bring the country to normalcy after liberation. According to the Agreement, all Greek Forces, such as the National Army and all the resistance groups, were placed under the temporary allied command by a British officer. The Caserta's Agreement comprised also the following:

«1. All the rebel groups in Greece are due to obey the orders of the Greek government of National Union.

2. The Greek government places these forces under the command of General Scobie, who was named by the Supreme Allied Commander, as the General of the Armed Forces in Greece.

3. According to the proclamation issued by the Greek government, the leaders of the Greek guerrillas would forbid all attempts of the Units to come to power; such an action will be considered a crime and will be punished accordingly.

4. As far as Athens is concerned, no action will be taken except under the direct orders of General Scobie, General Governor of the Greek Forces.

5. Security Battalions are regarded as enemy groups; they will be considered as enemies unless they obey the orders of the Greek forces, rather than of their General Administrator.

6. All the Greek Forces, to end up the conflicts of the past, declare that they will form a National Union to coordinate their actions for the best interest of their common struggle.

7. Following the acknowledgment by the Supreme Council of Commons and in a Consensus with the Greek government, General Scobie issued his orders:

- The Chief General of the Greek Armed Forces explained his purpose in which the country's reconstruction would be undertaken by the Greek government and material support would be given to people.

- As far as the current Armed Forces in Greece are concerned, their organization will be the following: a. General Zervas will continue to operate within the territorial boundaries of Plaka's Agreement and will work with General Sarafis to harass the German retreat within the area between the northern boundaries of Plaka and Albanian territory, b. General Sarafis will continue to operate in the rest of Greece, except for:

I. Region of Attica - all the troops in this region will be governed by General Spiliotopoulos (acting in close cooperation with the members of the government in Athens and assisted by an Associated officer who will be named by General Sarafis) - they will be under the command of Force 140;

II. Peloponnese - the troops in this region will be run by an officer (who will be named by General Sarafis after the Greek government's approval), and who will be assisted by an English Liaison Mission - they will be under the command of Force 140;

III. Thrace (including Thessaloniki) - will be under the command of an officer named by the Greek government.

- *Aims:*
    a. Both Governors will harass the German retreat and deactivate the German Guard,

b. By the time that the territory will be liberated, both Commanders will be personally responsible to govern Bounty 140 for keeping law and order in the lands where their forces are operating; avoiding the civil war and the murders of Greeks to Greeks; failing to impose any penalties and unjustified arrests; contributing to the restoration of legitimate political power and distributing care.
- A map showing the boundaries of the operations was given to both Commanders».

The withdrawal of Germans

On the 6th of July 1944, the Allies disembarked in Normandy. It was now evident in Greece that the iron German discipline had been disturbed. There were everywhere conflicting orders and Germans began to behave like the Italians at the time of their capitulation. In the streets and squares of Athens, Germans sold furniture, weapons, ammunition and various devices, e.g. typewriters, while they were buying political clothes and footwear. Also, desertions began just like the accession of some German soldiers to ELAS on the mountains, where they became instructors of the guerrillas on German weapons. In August 1944 Germans decided to abandon Greece and transfer their forces from Greece back to Germany.

It has been written that on the 1st of September 1944, an Agreement was signed in Livadi, Thessaloniki, between Captain Kitsos, commander of the 2nd Order of the 31st Constitution of ELAS, as representative of the Division of Macedonia guerrillas, and the Major Erich Fenske, Commander of Unit 31756, as representative of the German Armed Forces of the Aegean. With this agreement, ELAS pledged among others not to prevent the German army from leaving the Macedonia area, as well as to enter any evacuation area only after the arrival of the last German soldier. The German Supreme Military Administration of Mace-donia pledged to order the withdrawal of the Anti-communist SBs from Thessaloniki and hand it over to

ELAS reserves and EAM political organization. However, leftist writers deny the existence of such an Agreement.

ELAS' men sometimes were troubling Germans quite a lot, yet most of the time left them undisturbed or undertook only some symbolic actions! It seems that ELAS did not want to have losses before the critical time that Siantos intended the seizure of power. On the 15th of November, the British officers ascertained ELAS's actions against the other resistance groups and hence decided to stop supplying it.

The British forces (both aviation and navy) were also subdued in dealing with German troops in Greece at that time. The rationale was (quite probable) that British preferred that Germans return to the north of the Balkan Peninsula to prevent Russians from descending to the Aegean areas.

At last, the confirmation came: Mathiopoulos in his book «The Greek Resistance and the Allies», the German Minister of Hitler's Armaments Cabinet, Albert Speer, quotes: «I remember that General Jondle, the head of the German Staff, came one day and told me that there was an agreement at high level between England and Germany concerning Greece. The agreement, unknown until then and unique to the Second World War, concerned in accordance with Jondle the evacuation of Greece from the German troops that will happen without British interference»! However, the British saboteurs in Greece demonstrated strong activity in the operation «Kivotos» as they destroyed trains and railways and attacked German shelters and bridges. Moreover, the departing Germans destroyed many bridges, rail tunnels, and railway stations so they could not be used by the Allies and sank several ships in the country's major ports and the Corinthian Canal to prevent their use for a few months. At the end of the war, three-quarters of the country's merchant fleet and all planes had been destroyed. In this setting, Piraeus' port was blasted, while Thessaloniki's port was rescued due to the intercession of Bishop Gennadios to the German authorities. On the 27th of August 1944, the German

3. The National Resistance 1941-1944

troops retreated from Greece with a daily departure of six trains with army and supplies. In September 1944 the Police Chief in Athens Angelos Evert was for a while the transitional Commander of Athens. Then, General N. Spiliotopoulos was appointed by the exiled government on the 19th of September as the military Commander of Attica before all Germans depart. At the end of September 1944, a three-member delegation of Ministers from the Papandreou's government arrived in Greece; they were politicians Manouilidis, Zevgos, and Tsatsos, and circulated the following orders:

a. it was forbidden to grant asylum to persons who had participated in occupying governments or had taken office during Occupation, b. everything left by the enemy belonged to the Greek state, c. it was forbidden to issue political newspapers with titles used during the Occupation as well as during the dictatorship, d. Aristides Skleros was appointed interim Mayor, e. the Bank of Greece remained closed until new banknotes could be printed.

On the 11th of October 1944, British paratroopers fell in Megara, but they were not involved in a battle with Germans. On the morning of the 12th of October, a German delegation officially handed the city over to the Mayor Angelos Georgatos and deposited kindly a wreath of laurel at the monument of the Unknown Soldier. General Felmy had already declared Athens as an imperial (protected) city and had asked for assurances that the Greeks would not attack the departing Germans. Under this agreement, the Marathon Dam and the Electric Company were not blown. Nevertheless, it was necessary for Greeks to fight with fanatic Germans to save the Dam as well as with the intervention of the National Resistance Organization «National Action» and Tomashauseen, the philhellene director of the Electric Company threw the explosives into the sea. On the 3rd of November 1944, the last German soldiers crossed the Greek border. As soon as Germans left Athens, the Athenians rushed into the streets. However, the ELAS started to take initiatives despite having no authorization for these. They began arbitrarily to tax commercial shops in gold pounds or any other kind, mainly food. Thus, traders were terrified and closed their shops to be secure. Moreover, the KKE's teams with red banners shouted slogans and were constantly circulating the streets.

On the 15th of October 1944, in response to EAM-ELAS events, a large demonstration was organized by National Organizations (PEAN, EDES, National Action and others) at the pillars of Olympian Zeus (Athens centre) with the participation of non-communist people. The slogan that was prevailing was «Great Greece», but fanatic leftists interrupted the demonstration, protested at the demonstrators and (according to Zalokosta's memories) attacked the crowd with boards. In general, incidents between EAM-ELAS and rivalry among the non-left national organizations became daily events.

The battle of Meligalas between Greeks

After the Germans' withdrawal, Peloponnese was controlled by the 2nd ELAS Division with a total force of 6,000 men who were led by Aris Velouchiotis. Then, executions of dissidents (against the Monarch-Fascists according to KKE's terminology) took place in a number that varies among publications. Meligalas was the seat of the 3rd SBs (Kalamata-Meligalas), whose forces had been previously terrorized by the local EAM fans. Following the Germans' withdrawal, on the 5th of September 1944, 200 gendarmes, State Officials and many other men of the SBs remained in Kalamata. On the 9th of September, ELAS led by Captain Nikos Beloyiannis, attacked Kalamata. The forces of the SBs then comprised of 900 men; gendarmes, right-wing citizens with their families, as well as Messinia's Prefect D. Perrotis and various Mayors and Anti-communists resorted to Meligalas where they felt safer. ELAS forces comprised of 1,200 armed men with heavy weapons. They attacked Meligalas and after a three-day raging battle with

3. The National Resistance 1941-1944

victims on both sides, ELAS' men finally intruded the city. Pillages and retaliation massacres followed. Aris Velouchiotis who was far away had ordered in advance that all captured men would have had to be killed. Thus, between the 15th and the 20th of September 1944, severe crimes had taken place. Prisoners, even entire families who had gone to Meligalas to protect themselves from ELAS, were moved at two kilometers outside the city, where there was a natural cavity of about 8 meters in diameter and 17 meters in depth, which was called «well». At that place the non-communists were executed in various ways —usually not with bullets— and their bodies were thrown into the well. It is reported that many corpses were found horribly crippled. The whole process lasted four days. Young people, boys, and girls, aged 16-17 years old were also murdered. Various villagers witnessed the horrible crimes, others remained due to their sympathy to EAM-ELAS and others remained there compulsorily for exemplification. Elias Theodoropoulos recorded 1,154 dead, while ELAS reported that 60 guerrillas (ELAS) and 800 men of the SBs were killed. Moreover, some Gendarmerie officers and brigands were transferred to Kalamata Square, where they were abused and eventually killed. The communists hated the gendarmes because they were hunting them, thanks to the law «idionymon» (1929, of the Eleftherios Venizelos government); this tactic continued during Metaxa's dictatorship as well as during the pseudo state of the foreign occupation. It has to be noted that General Sarafis referred only to «*enemy losses of 800 people in the field of battle of Meligalas*» in his book «ELAS»; yet, in this way, a biased story was written by Sarafis for this massacre.

According to Prof. S. Kalivas, about 55% of the victims were killed by EAM and 45% by Germans and the SBs in Argolida. According to a (left) report, the total of killings was committed by right-wing guerrilla groups in the period from the 12th of February 1945 to the 31st of March 1946 across the country accounted to 1,289, which were approximately only the victims of ELAS in the prefectures of Argos and Corinthos. The «price» of the new National Discord was really heavy. On the 27th of September, the representative of the P. Kanellopoulos government, showing extraordinary courage went to Peloponnese and met in Kalamata with Aris Velouchiotis. He persuaded the SBs of Peloponnese to abandon their weapons and they had to be transported to an island for their safety. P. Kanellopoulos writes for this period: «The largest region of Greece even before the Germans left had been conquered with the help of Western allies (including their forces and money) from EAM-ELAS. Therefore, the exclusive control was in the hands of the communists. When the Germans started to depart from the southwestern Peloponnese, ELAS instead of chasing Germans (who had rarely been seriously confronted by them) entered the cities and began massacres and torture; hence, over six thousand Greeks died in the first weeks of September 1944».

Criticism for the National Resistance

Nowadays, nearly a century after the events, we must put a critical viewpoint against the actions of the National Resistance 1942-1944. It is evident that significant actions took place against the enemies, which had a psychological impact on the morale of the occupational forces in Greece; on the contrary, the Hellenic morale was enhanced by such actions, i.e. the blast of the National - Socialist Party building in Athens, the blast of Gorgopotamos bridge and Asopos bridge, as well as the attack to the Kastelli airport, the sabotaging activities of Ivanov and Adam, etc. However, the villages and residents of the surrounding areas had serious implications out of several resistance actions. There were reprisals with executions of many villagers or hostages for each German soldier who was killed by the rebels, as well as house fires; entire villages were

3. The National Resistance 1941-1944

destroyed by such reprisals. The British wanted the Resistance interfering with the Germans in order to retain significant forces in Greece, which would be used on other fronts. In fact, the additional forces that were needed for the Germans to fight the resistance groups in the mountains, were only two divisions. On the other hand, the presence of British agents in the Greek mountains included political significance. Moreover, there is belief that the British deliberately reinforced ELAS in order to create a civil conflict so that Greece ultimately would not claim anything for its participation in the war, namely the Dodecanese, Northern Epirus, and Cyprus). Another explanation is that SOE was sympathizing the leftist, despite the different views of Churchill and Eden who were responsible for the British policy.

As far as the Resistance groups, they were formed by the entire political spectrum; yet, the senior politicians of the large parties did not participate. The KKE, having the experience of being for many years outlawed, had a great tactical advantage. EAM included all the communists, the socialists Svolos and Tsirimokos, as well as many non-communists at the beginning. However, the communists were guiding the policy of EAM, and all of EAM's leaders decisions were essentially the decisions of the KKE. Later, when ELAS was established by Velouchiotis, the connection between EAM-ELAS and the KKE began to appear, despite the initial KKE's intention to hide this connection. Ultimately, the members of ELAS were accepting the «communist enlightenment» every day and sang guerrilla songs according to Soviet music scales. ELAS gained many guerrillas due to EAM's attraction, a fact that was appreciated by the British and it was heavily reinforced with money and weapons, while the other organizations –except for EDES, which was also reinforced– were asking for help in vain. Military help with parachutes, including ammunition, clothing, and gold pounds was a good reason for ELAS to fight against all other resistance organizations. When the political objectives of EAM-

ELAS became apparent, non-communist organizations began to view ELAS guerrillas as rivals who intended to establish a communist regime in Greece by the force of arms. So, distrust and rivalry were developed. From spring 1943 onwards, most armed conflicts occurred among the Greek resistance groups rather than against Germans.

As more the number of ELAS men grew, the more everyone else was growing worried as to what would happen in the future. Sarafis in his autobiography wrote that «*the forces of EDES or other organizations attacked ELAS*»; however, this can only be accepted as an exception. Moreover, it is obvious ELAS as the larger organization could attack easily the weaker groups. Furthermore, ELAS aggressiveness increased when they took over the best quality armament from the Italian Pinerolo Division in September 1943. When the ELAS pressure was increased, many of the non-communists began to accept German ammunition to defend themselves. The non-communists saw the danger coming from the left (EAM-ELAS) during the time the Germans were preparing to leave. The SBs then came along with their detours, while contributing to the confrontation of communists. Greece in 1943-1944 felt like a powder keg and sooner or later the explosion would happen. In those days, there was common mistrust between ELAS and the Papandreou government. It has also to be noted that the «Siamese organization» of EAM-ELAS-KKE those days held the power.

Professor Stathis Kalivas in an article published in Kathimerini newspaper (5-8-2011) wrote the following: «The greatest benefit of the resistance is recorded at the symbolic level (...) the resistance failed in most of its objectives, while its cost to the country was great (...) Greece has not liberated thanks to the resistance (...) the resistance was connected to a civil war». Naturally, such a brave opinion was first expressed by General N. Plastiras at the Meeting of the 25th of December 1944. Moreover, regardless what was said or was written, the crucial

3. The National Resistance 1941-1944

issues in 1944, were mainly the political as well as the state status of the country by the departure of the Germans, and not the resistance against them, since it was obvious that −sooner or later− they would leave the country. As a consequence, the Greeks in 1943 and 1944 were unfortunately deeply divided once again.

The Agreement of influence percentages

On the 9th of October 1944, British Prime Minister Churchill met with Russian leader Joseph Stalin and agreed upon an amazing Pact on «the control rates they would have in the liberated countries» after the defeat of Germans. Greece would be in the sphere of British influence by 90%. Obviously, due to these British-ESSR inter-service relations, the Russian troops that entered Bulgaria stopped at the Greek-Bulgarian borders, despite that KKE pleaded to Russians to moving forward so as to establish a Soviet-style People's Democracy» in Greece. It seems that these agreements «on the spheres of influence» were possibly not known to Greek communists.

Chapter 4

THE LIBERATION OF GREECE

The Greek government and the British in Athens

Since early October, the first British troops had begun disembarking on the coasts of the western Peloponnese, according to Caserta Agreement. Bartziotas, as Chief of ELAS' reservist union, was eager to take power in a «coup d' état». But after the Lebanon and Caserta Agreements, KKE's policy had changed and was in favor of maintaining order and participating in the government. The strong KKE's leaders, Siantos and Ioannidis, approved this change of political line.

The exiled Greek government along with British forces under General Scobie arrived in Athens on the 18th of October 1944. Papandreou raised the Greek flag on the Acropolis and immediately participated in a mass at the cathedral under Archbishop Damaskinos. There were problems in the church because the opposing sides were whispering in the temple against each other. Thereafter, the Prime Minister delivered a speech at Syntagma Square in a crowd mainly by an EAM-KKE as derived by the red flags and respective slogans such as «Laocracy; not the King». To impassion his audience, Papandreou said to his speech *that «we believe in the government by the people (laocratia)»*. He was then accused of this saying by his political opponents; however, perhaps at that moment, that slogan was necessary. He also referred to the issue of «*National Integration*» (Northern Epirus-Dodecanese and to the settlement of safe northern borders), the need to re-establish the Armed Forces and the Security Corpses, and imposing sanctions to the «collaborators». Moreover, he emphasized the need to restore the functioning of the liberated Greek State following the Lebanon and Kazerta Agreements and signed by the political parties, EAM and EDES. He also referred to the Rimini Brigade, the «Sacred Company» and the resistance of Athenians and he ended his speech stressing the need for *«national unity»,* allied with the main slogan of the Papandreou government was *«one Country; one Government; one Army».*

One of the first actions of Papandreou's government was to take over the SBs. The SBs members who made crimes, as well as the members of the occupying (pseudo) governments, were jailed: in total 600 collaborators and among them the two former Prime Ministers (Tsolakoglou and Rallis) and as many of the former Ministers were found and were imprisoned. It must be noted that the former Prime Minister Logothepoulos, the former Vice President Tsironikos and the former Minister of Finance Gotzamanis had managed to flee to Germany.

With the decision to form a National Guards Division, the first frictions within the government were created because the Undersecretary of Interior Lambrianidis, arbitrarily appointed only right-wing officers as Executives. In consequence, Papandreou abolished Lambrianidis, put in Ministry P. Sariyannis (a leftist General from EAM) and he also instructed three left-wing Ministers to form the protocol of demobilization of all rebel groups.

The 3rd Mountain Brigade, which had fought bravely in Italy's Rimini, led by General T. Tsakalotos, disembarked on the 8th of November 1944 in Piraeus and organized a parade in Athens, where he was applauded. The KKE wanted to abolish the Brigade since this unit was formed in the Middle East by right-wing men. However, Tsakalotos refused to move the Brigade from Goudi to Parnitha (outside Athens), saying: *«The Brigade will not leave Athens at the mercy of the communists».* On the 9th of November 1944, Churchill sent a note to Eden, saying: *«Definitely, I am expecting a conflict with EAM, which we must not avoid provided the field is properly selected ...we should not have hesitations to use the British army to support the Greek government of G. Papandreou».* On the 4th of November 1944, EAM gave an oath which aimed to *«...Greece to seek complete liberation from the foreign burden»* and on the 7th of November, a statement was issued asking *«...ELAS to launch the final fight».* All that time, Stalin complied with his Agreement with Churchill and he was primarily interested to arrange the communist regime in Romania. Papandreou sought to disarm all the guerrillas so as to make it possible to go for elections. He intended to form a new National Army Brigade by ELAS men and another by EDES men together with the 3rd Mountain Brigade and Sacred Company of C. Tsigantes. Thus, while the disarmament of the rebel units was agreed, EAM ministers returned the next day and insisted on dis-armament of the Rimini 3rd Mountain Brigade and Sacred Company. On the 2nd of December 1944, the ministers of EAM resigned from Papandreou's government. EAM-ELAS considered the arrival of the British in Greece as an interference with the internal affairs of the country. Therefore EAM (actually the KKE) was aiming for a frontal collision with the civil state. Of course, they didn't think that the British troops would be involved in a civil conflict.

The battle of Athens in December 1944 – «Dekembriana»

G. Papandreou and the British agents suspected that ELAS intended to attack Athens to seize power. The British officers who were in the mountains and cooperated with the guerrillas were the first ones to suspect ELAS' intentions. In July 1944 N.

Hammond had already informed Cairo's Headquarters that *«...Siantos' scope is to occupy Athens and Thessaloniki, exterminate his opponents and establish a communist State»*. Moreover, ELAS ordered man-datory recruitment of men in villages and cities where there were no longer remaining Germans. It is important to note that ELAS already had enough forces; Anti-Fascist or opportunist Germans were even accepted to serve as instructors of its men to find the German weapons that were held. However, for unknown reasons, ELAS did not attack Athens as soon as Germans left, but it took about two months for this to happen. Probably Siantos either was afraid of a subsequent involvement of British forces, or he waited for Stalin's consent, which was not coming since Stalin had other priorities at that time. He probably even was waiting for a good excuse for the conflict, so that he could have the public's positive opinion.

ELAS still had numerical superiority in Attica. However, Siantos made the mistake of sending Sarafis and Velouchiotis against Zervas in Epirus. On the 1st of December 1944, ELAS of Macedonia attacked against the forces of Anton Tsaous (Fostiridis) in Drama and the forces of Michalagas in Kozani. It has to be noted that along with the resignation of EAM's ministers, parts of ELAS' forces gathered very close to Athens, despite Scobie's orders to avoid cities. The forces that Siantos could use were about 22,000 men. In the other forces of ELAS that were with Sarafis and Velouchiotis were about 60,000 men and they were fighting in Epirus to exterminate EDES and the other small armed non-communist Hellenic groups. Moreover, a Division led by Markos Vafiadis and E. Bakirtzis was in Thessaloniki.

On the 1st of December 1944, ELAS men were ordered to gather around the Police Stations of Athens and Piraeus ready for the fight which had been planned long ago. The KKE abandoned its offices in Athens, a fact indicating that the conflict was imminent. The orders were given by Siantos, who

4. The Liberation of Greece

was the one to begin the conflict. Thus, on the same day that the ELAS Revolutionary Committee was reassembled, Siantos as the Leader released a secret order. The plan was to exterminate the 3rd Mountain Brigade in Goudi, to encircle and disarm the Police Stations, to seize bridges to prevent their use by the «enemy forces», to occupy hills to control the areas nearby, to clear Thysseon from organization X of colonel G. Grivas as well as the Vathis' square area from the motorized police battalion under Colonel Buradas, and to act against the Headquarters of the Police's General Security. According to the plan, there was no provision for the British involvement in this project. On the 2nd of December, ELAS men were commanded to prevent police officers from leaving their headquarters. Also were commanded to attack against the 3rd Mountain Brigade. Zevgos, who was one of the resigned KKE's ministers, published an article in Rizospastis newspaper writing: *«... the negotiation time is over»* and that *«... only weapons can solve the differences»!* The Socialists, Svolos and Tsirimokos, were pressed psychologically by KKE men and therefore they were unable to react; their resignation from the Minister's posts meant that they were protesting against both the left and right political factions.

It is easily concluded from all the above that Siantos (KKE, EAM, ELAS) intended to attack the government and its «reactionary» supporters, as soon as he thought that the time was right, having found a good excuse for this action. On the 3rd of December, EAM had planned a political rally in the center of Athens and a general strike the day after. The Papandreou government initially allowed the rally to take place, but shortly after decided to halt it, because the Police had information that episodes were about to occur. On the morning of the 3rd of December 1944, men of Organization X fought with ELAS men who had occupied the hill of Philopapou. Before the rally, a group of protesters attacked the guards of the Prime Minister's home, as written in General Scobie's diary: *«...a group of protesters threw two bullets outside Papandreou's home at Vasilissis Sofias Street and killed two Police officers...».*

Inevitably, the rally took place despite the ban and the protesters headed towards Constitution Square. The demonstrators disarmed a few policemen. A group of protesters moved towards the Athens Police Headquarters (at the corner of Panepistimiou and Vasilissis Sophias Street), but when they came close enough, the Policemen started shooting. According to Scobie's diary: *«...When the protesters attempted to break the police ring in the Square, and the protesters started grabbing the policemen's guns, the policemen shot initially in the air. At that point, a Greek military officer appeared with a Tomigan (automatic weapon) and started shooting towards the crowd. He was the one who caused most death».*

ELAS occupied the Police Stations in Piraeus and attacked against the united Headquarters of the British and Greek Navy».

Generally, as described in many related publications «...*somebody shot at some point, but it is unknown from which side».* The right-wing MP N. Farmakis mentioned in an interview that Police Chief Captain Angel Evert gave the signal by shaking a handkerchief from a window to the Police officers in the streets as a signal when to shoot. Many years later, Angel Evert in one of his interviews accepted that he was the one who gave the signal to the Police officers to shoot, as he was following the government's instructions. This decision was made because the protesters were a threat to the Police Headquarters and they had already disarmed a few Policemen. In any case, it does not matter which side started the conflict because there was mutual distrust, and this event was inevitable. Furthermore, this event was predetermined and organ-ized in advance by the KKE, and hence expected; armed men were anyway among the protesters. It is now evident that the KKE via ELAS had planned to attack Athens, as proven by a series of objective data.

4. The Liberation of Greece

Of course, we can remark that if during the occupation years the KKE and EAM-ELAS were not so aggressive to anyone who was not lining up with them, therefore the non-communists would probably had not confronted them. EAM initially was attacking Germans and their collaborators, but after mid-1943 it began attacking anyone who was thought to be «reactionary»; this implied anyone who was not registered in EAM in line with Siantos's statement. According to Ioannidis, *«there was also a decision by the Politburo that we would go there (in conflict) if we do not find any other solution»*. Also, according to Ioannidis, *«...we (KKE) were proceeding, according to a plan, to find a reason for the war to begin»*. According to Secretary of EAM, Chatzis, *«... Siantos, not so much theoretically, but with his revolutionary instinct and his tremendous experience, had realized that weapons, with their dynamically executed powers, give control and stabilization»*.

As far as the Constitution Square events are concerned, it is certain that the victims were many, while the Policemen did shoot. Related publications reported different numbers of deaths, but they were much less than what one would expect from the numerous shots given. Apparently, some shots were given in the air to frighten their opponents. Thus, the Constitution Square soon emptied from the protesters who ran to save themselves. Dead bodies and the wounded protesters were left on the ground. Panagiotis Kanellopoulos reported that there were 11 deaths; in other reliable British sources, 16 deaths are mentioned. However, the following day EAM organized a funeral with 24 coffins (some of them were probably empty or contained stones!). Miltiadis Evert, who was the son of Police officer A. Evert, in a letter to newspaper «Vima» on the 19th of December 1980, wrote that *«the conflict started when unarmed, as well as armed protesters, climbed on the railings of the police station and while being in a clash with the police officers, they were the ones who shot first and killed a policeman near the gate; immediately afterward, A. Evert ordered the Policemen to shoot too»*. Other sources also reported that at first a Policeman was killed by a grenade. Siantos' orders to begin the operation were given on the 3rd of December. The funerals on the following day after the episodes were fully organized and it was also the excuse for additional episodes. Thus, men from Organization X shot from hotel windows around Omonia Square towards the funeral crowd.

These bloody events and their consecutive 33 days of battles in Athens are called «Dekembriana». At that time, ELAS practically owned all of Athens, except for a small area downtown. During the first two days of the battles, the British remained neutral and acted more as a referee. Papandreou telegrammed his resignation to King George in London. Spyros Markezinis, as the informal representative of King George, was negotiating even before the events of December with the old politician Sofoulis and suggested to the British that Sofoulis becomes Prime Minister. But that was not a decision that King George could take alone; Churchill had to agree as well. Markezinis also called for Sofoulis' commitment, to deny the designation of a Regent. The negotiations were made with the former Chief-priest of «Evangelismos», David Balfour[4], who

---

[4] David Balfour was a very interesting personality. While a Catholic monk in the order of the Benedictines, he converted to Orthodoxy and was ordained as monk Demetrius on Mount Athos (1932). His spiritual guides were the Russian Abbot Silouan and the archimandrite Sofronios. He learned Greek and Russian in Greece but also spoke Italian, French, German, Polish and Turkish. He studied at the Theological School of the National Kapodistrian University of Athens, became a monk in the Penteli monastery, was ordained a priest and soon assumed the title of archimandrite. It was based at Evangelismos' Hospital in Athens, where he organized an excellent choir, had friendly relations with the Athens Palace, its elite and was confessor to many Athenians and palace officials, perhaps even to King George. Prior to the departure of the British military and diplomats from Greece in 1941, he was in Egypt where he took off his clothes, shaved his beards and served as a military officer. He returned to Athens in 1944 and in December became a diplomat in close cooperation with the Ambassador Lepper, even residing at the British Embassy. He had

4. The Liberation of Greece

was then a diplomatic officer, under the direct supervisor of Ambassador Reginald Leeper. At the end, Sofoulis proceeded to become Prime Minister of a coalition government but Churchill didn't want to deal with political intrigues, because at that time he was focusing on ELAS' danger; thus, he insisted that Papandreou remains the Prime Minister. The number of British and governmental forces at that time was about 20% of the respective ELAS men. Siantos, a former tobacco worker (and former sergeant in the army) was in charge of the Battle in Athens. He became the Head of the 3rd Division of Peloponnese, of the 2nd and 13th Brigades in middle Greece, and of the Brigade of the Thessalian Cavalry. Sarafis became the Captain of the 1st and 8th Epirus Divisions as well as the Captain of four Brigades in northern Greece, in order to attack EDES in Epirus, and Michalagas' group in western Macedonia. On the 3rd of December, the Battle of Thysseon, an area in Athens close to Acropolis, began. Eighty Fighters of Organization X were distributed at selected positions. Another 40 men of Organization X were in a premise on Solonos street. On the 4th of December, ELAS' attack was launched, and a great battle took place. The men of X, (among them were a lot of Army officers), fought valiantly in Thysseon from the dawn till the afternoon, when they were forced to stop fighting and leave, due to the lack of ammunition. By then, about half of them were

---

frequent contacts and political consultations with Spyros Markezinis and Themistocles Sofoulis until the referendum and King George's return to Athens. Many consider him to be a spy for Britain. It is most likely that he served his country when needed. He served as a diplomat at the British Foreign Office in Israel, the Consulate of Izmir and Geneva. But his relationship with Orthodoxy - after intense dubiousness - continued even after his secularization and his marriage. Until his death, he continued to pray and associate with the Immaculate Mysteries. Often in churches he read the Symbol of Faith. Occasionally exchanged letters with Sophronios contained in an Elderly book entitled "The Struggle for Theology". He wrote the theological poem of Saint Simeon the Archbishop of Thessaloniki (1416 / 17-1429).

either killed or wounded. The British helped all survivors to leave from Thysseon into military cars. Several survivors went to the Gendarmerie camp of Makrygianni or to the National Guards. Siantos ordered the A' Army Corps of ELAS to occupy the Police Stations. The 2nd Brigade in Attica with its 2nd Squad (Papazisis as the Commander Major and Nikiforos as the Captain) would attack the 3rd Rimini Mountain Brigade. However, a strong force of British armored vehicles managed to nonviolently disarm Nikiforos' men and hence his men were sent to Thebes. Moreover, on the 4th of December, other conflicts of protesters and Nationalists took also place in Omonia Square, with many victims. Scobie ordered all members of ELAS to leave Athens within 72 hours and Sarafis replied that Scobie had to communicate on that with ELAS' Central Committee. However, on the same day as well as the following one, a general attack of ELAS against Police Stations took place and lead to massacres of a lot of Police officers; ELAS' men killed the arrested policemen by cutting their carotids with knives to save bullets!

In cases where Police officers surrendered after negotiations, they were immediately disarmed and released. However, there were cases when the ELAS men did not keep their promises and killed them, anyway. During that time, ELAS also tried to occupy the «Averof Prison», where the former Prime Minister I. Rallis along with 500 collaborators were imprisoned, but they were overcome by British and by two units from the Rimini Brigade. However, the former minister General Bakos was arrested and was soon executed after a short trial by EAM-ELAS. Additionally, they took over the prison on Vouliagmeni Street from which they captured 38 Police officers and gendarmes and executed them after two days.

On the 5th of December, Churchill gave Scobie an order that the British should attack ELAS and prevail in Athens, to which he referred to as an «occupied city». Moreover, Churchill urged Marshal Wilson to support Scobie. Churchill said: «*I do*

4. The Liberation of Greece

not care what will happen to Bologna but (I care about) Athens» and *«Athens must be held without or even with bloodshed».* After the events of December, more of ELAS' Units started to move to Athens and the British stopped them by using a brief air attack. On the 6th of December, ELAS's men tried to occupy the Ministry of Interior, but they were forced to leave. After this, the British were not acting as referees anymore but began fighting aligning with the forces of the Greek government.

On the 6th of December, early in the morning, the «Regimen of Gendarmerie Makrygiannis» were forcefully attacked. The gendarmes bravely defended themselves, though they had many losses. Moreover, gendarmes from outposts that were located outside the camp and inside apartment buildings were eventually arrested and the survivors executed. At one crucial point, three British tanks were sent to assist the defenders. Eventually, seven days later, ELAS men decided to give up. At this stage, the 3rd Mountain Brigade began protecting some important public buildings in the center of Athens. During the night the 3rd Mountain Brigade was attacked by ELAS. The experienced warriors of Rimini dealt with this attack calmly. Tsakalotos then accepted to have the SBs' officers at his service, knowing that if any of these officers got arrested, he would surely be executed. Among them, he accepted Colonel Papadongonas, whom he truly respected but he was killed soon

Meanwhile, the 2nd National Division had formed and already two opposing factions existed: the communists and on the opposite side everyone else, i.e. Democrats socialists, Centrists, Right-wingers, Ultra-conservatives and even collaborators of the Germans. The member of EDES Colonel Leonidas Spais was the one who took over the responsibility for the SBs, replacing the leftist Deputy Secretary Sariyannis on the 7th of December. During these days, Tsakalotos wrote that «free Athens consisted of two squares and five streets».

The 3rd Greek Mountain Brigade secured the road from Syntagma to the coast of Faliro, where the 139 British Brigade was active, and at the same time cleared the areas of Zografou - Ano Ilissia and occupied the eastern part of the Kessariani hill. On the 9th of December, ELAS, after the initiation of Zevgos' attacked the Hellenic Military Academy, where there were 23 military officers and 183 pilots. However, the British army interfered and allowed the surrounded to leave. On the 11th of December, when the Makrygiannis Regimen was at risk, Major General Arkreit of the British 23rd Armoured Brigade, suggested that the governmental forces and the British ought to escape with ships. However, Colonel T. Tsakalotos reacted promptly by saying «no way; the Brigade shall not retreat; it will defend itself right to the end of our homeland», and hence his men remained to their positions. By all means, their retreat would have contributed to their discouragement. During that time, several army officers took weapons and formed a new battalion as soldiers.

On the same day, the British General Alexander and the Minister McMillan came to Athens as responsible for Mediterranean affairs. Churchill had told Alexander *«peace will only come after a victory»*. The two men were using a battle tank for their transport; with it they arrived at the building where Scobie was stationed (they could only see what was happening outside with a periscope!). The situation, as Scobie exposed it, was tragic. ELAS owned 4/5 of Athens and Piraeus as well as the airport in Tatoi, while men of RAF were isolated in a hotel at Kifissia. Seventeen out of the 23 police stations in Athens were occupied by ELAS. Aid could only come through the Faliron coast, which was partly controlled by British troops. The Chief General Alexander then called General John Hawksworth to come from Italy along with his Executives. He proved to be very good at his job in comparison to Scobie who was unexperienced and had not run a combat Unit. This British General also made sure that aid was sent comprising a British

4. The Liberation of Greece

and an Indian Division. Scobie woud have a role in political affairs; he was rather deemed to be inadequate in military affairs, but he was not withdrawn from duty.

On the 13th of December very early in the morning, strong ELAS' forces attacked a British camp (in an area called Parapigmata). Many British trucks were exploded there because they were filled with ammunition. In the morning the Greek 3rd Mountain Brigade and the Aviation attacked ELAS' men. As a result, ELAS guerrillas were repelled to Ampelokipi and hence the British heavy ammunition was rescued. On the 14th of December, another battle took place with soldiers who occupied Kastela. On the 16th and 17th of December, new British aid landed in Faliro and re-occupied areas of Athens owned by ELAS. On the same day, 2,500 men (5 Battalions) of the newly-formed Ethnic Guard participated in street battles. The British sought and gained full control of Singrou Avenue, which was used for transferring soldiers from Faliro to the center of Athens. During the night on the 17th of December, ELAS' forces took over three hotels in Kifissia, where RAF personnel were staying. Moreover, they captured 585 British, officers, maintainers and infantries. In general, street battles were still going on in various areas in Athens. British tanks were attempting to break up the barricades and ELAS' members were trying to deal with them without having any anti-tank weapons. When the weather allowed, the British Air Force would take action. Thus, on the 18th December, the British occupied Lycabettus hill, from where they were able to observe many highways and control them. Moreover, one Ethnic Guard Battalion was already attached to every British Battalion. During the night of the 23rd of December ELAS' men placed explosives into underground pipelines near Great Britain Hotel, where the Greek government and the British Staff were based. The explosion was postponed due to the arrival of Churchill in Greece. Meanwhile, the British discovered and destroyed the explosives.

During the battles in Athens, ELAS arrested many citizens as hostages, including the widow of John Metaxas and a lot of people living in rich neighborhoods i.e. Generals, admirals, intellectuals, publishers, doctors, lawyers, judges, former ministers, university professors, and merchants. However, many other citizens were arrested as well. All of them, in total about 30,000 people, were forced to walk through Central Greece in very cold weather. Some other groups of hostages were transported to Lamia by cars. As a result, as it was reported the total number of deaths was about 1,200 people. In general, some hostages died from the hardships, others were executed because they were slow in walking due to their physical weakness from illness or old age. Some hostages were selected either to exchange them with the captured of ELAS' men or to execute them. Two interesting descriptions of such hostages were written by Alexandra Kriezis and Metaxas' widow.

Those who arrived at Trikala, where Sarafis was, were all fed and survived at his assurance. The decision regarding the hostages was taken by the Political Bureau with the differentiation of Zevgos and Porphyrogenis. The KKE's rationale for capturing these hostages was that this was a counter-attack for the arrests of a few thousand ELAS guerrillas, whom the British had sent to the El Dhaba camp in Egypt. However, ELAS' hostages were arrested in advance and ELAS' guerrillas were transferred to Egypt several days later; thus, this excuse is unsubstantial.

Until the 25th of December, the British forces had increased significantly. They were reinforced with two divisions, a Brigade, and several Battalions. They also had airplanes, ships, and tanks at their disposal. British Prime Minister Churchill arrived in Athens on the 25th of December with USA's aircraft and he was transported on the warship «Ajax» to have discussions with Papandreou and Archbishop Damaskinos. A wider meeting was held on the 26th of December in the Ministry of Foreign Affairs

4. The Liberation of Greece

with just the lighting of oil lamps since the ELAS had cut off electricity. The communists came along later on with Siantos as their leader. Churchill spoke briefly to the representatives of all parties and asked Greeks to agree to make peace. In the meeting present were Papandreou, Plastiras, Eden, McMillan, the UK Ambassador Leeper, the USA Ambassador McBee, the French Ambassador Ballen, and the Russian Colonel Popov. After Churchill left the room, another consultation followed with the chair of Damaskinos, which was held between political leaders and the communists Siantos, Partsalidis and General Mantakas. At that meeting, Plastiras attacked the KKE and, inter alia, stated: *«I do not accept that the guerrilla parties liberated Greece; Greece was liberated from the course of the war»*. Later, after Siantos reacted by saying *«do not blame the resistance fighters»*. Plastiras said: *«I ask you this; why so many villages were burned in Greece? If rebels had to step out, they should have done it to save Greece, not to destroy it. And that's why I do not admit that they were the ones who liberated the country...»*. The meeting continued the next day with the presence of more politicians, yet it did not result in a positive outcome. Siantos was asking for almost half of the ministries of a newly formed administration; however, it was impossible for the politicians, the Papandreou's government as well as the British officers to agree on that. Moreover, ELAS was now the loser; thus, the superfluous of Siantos' demands was inexplicable.

On the 27th of December the British army, which at that moment had increased its weapons, launched a general assault on ELAS. On the 31st of December, the heavy firearms of the 3rd Mountain Brigade arrived in Athens. This Brigade cleared up Kessariani from the fighting ELAS men. Meanwhile, Churchill and Eden met in London with King George. After long talks, a telegram was sent to Papandreou, where the King declared that he had approved the appointment of Archbishop Damaskinos as Regent, *«... until the end of the current irregular state of affairs».* The King, retreating from his previous position, said that *«...I am determined to return to Greece after the free elections».*

The British did not plan to attack ELAS. However, Churchill had decided that Greece would remain in the Western sphere of influence, where countries with democratic parliamentary regimes belonged. And he wasn't willing to lose this fight. On the other hand, the British Prime Minister had his own difficulties because he had to face opposition in the Parliament and the reaction of the USA government, which could not understand why *«the British are attacking guerrillas who fought against Germans».* Interestingly, he responding to a question that was asked in the Parliament categorically that *«Britain is fighting for Democracy and ELAS for the dictatorship of the proletariat ... Democracy does not mean the law of the mob ... Democracy is not a prostitute that anyone with a Tommygun can shop on the street!».* Eventually, Churchill managed to get the vote of confidence for the British Army interventions in countries that were liberated from Germans.

At the end of December, *«the free area of the state around hotel Great Britain»* had expanded to *«the state of Athens and its surroundings»;*(according to Tsakalotos' memories). However, ELAS still owned the rest of the country.

The «Dekembriana» fights and everything else related to this nasty period of 33 days of Greek history have been characterized by the 11th Plenary Session of the KKE as *«...the diamond of our Nation's fight for the democratic reconstruction and independence of Greece...»!* But ELAS lost about 3,000 men, while other 3,500 men, including 474 officers, were killed on the governmental side along with some British men. Moreover, about 7,500 of the ELAS men were captured during Dekembriana. According to Sicle, the number of total losses in Greece from the 3rd of December to the 15th of January was up to 14,000 individuals. Later on, 25,000 leftists were arrested and were either imprisoned, or sent to concentration camps.

4. The Liberation of Greece

ELAS' men in principle executed everyone they had arrested after the fights. The Militia and OPLA (a special division of the communist Party of Greece), also executed many citizens who were considered by them as «reactive» or spies. On the contrary, the British did not execute the captives; there were about 18,000, while none of the captives of ELAS remained alive. In battles of December 1944, 30,000 citizens had been captured by ELAS to be used as hostages and most of them, though not all, remained alive.

The events of December 1944 and the «hostages» are the second round of the communist struggle to forcefully seize power. The first round was the civil conflicts of ELAS rebels with the non-left-wing resistance forces in 1943-1944 and the third round was the civil war of 1947-1949 that followed. The attempt of EAM-ELAS-KKE to seize power seems that had been organized previously. At a meeting of EAM politicians and ELAS troops in August 1943, a staffing plan for the occupation of Athens after the withdrawal of Germans, was organized by executive Major T. Makridis. In this case, the British army was not taken into account, so Bartziotas pointed out this and Makridis replied that *«if the English army will intervene, we would be lost»* The leader of the KKE G. Siantos fluctuated between co-operation with the political parties and the armed conflict with the «bourgeois state». In the former he wanted to participate in elections with the armed ELAS present; he thought that if elections were held with ELAS full of arms, they would win them. Since the decision of Papandreou about ELAS' dissolution has opened after the 27th of November, for the KKE the choice of conflict was the latter (plan B in today's terminology). The preparation of the KKE for a conflict with the opponents of the «bourgeoisie» had been planned as well as was the preparation of the non-communist leaders of Churchill and Papandreou. Mistrust was mutual and the dices were cast. Later, Bartziotas confirmed that the decision to occupy Athens had been taken since September.

The implementation of the final plan was left to the amateur «General» G. Siantos with the known subsequent results. Summing up, the Lebanon and Kazerta Agreements are cited as evidence against ELAS' plan to attack Athens and have been considered that are elements supporting the intention for a peaceful policy of the KKE. However, the KKE's representatives in Lebanon found themselves in a psychologically difficult position after the murder of Psarros and a number of his men and ELAS was continually dependent on Britain's help in the mountains. After the retreat in Lebanon, the KKE and EAM-ELAS was in difficulty at Caserta to declare rebels sabotaging the struggle of the British Allies against the Nazis.

The action of OPLA

During the Occupation and the subsequent 3-4 years, OPLA («Organization for the Protection of Folk Fighters» or «People's Struggle Protection Organization») murdered selected persons. OPLA was an organization entirely dependent on KKE, not related with EAM, mainly carrying out executions (murders) of individuals judged by its core nucleus as traitors, trumpeters and left-wing rivals of the KKE, like Archeomarxists, Trotskyists and Anarchists.

OPLA has mainly acted in Athens. In other cities, it acted as the «Acting Group» followed by the name of the city. In Thessaloniki, they were called «The People's Avengers», while after 1948 they changed their name to «The Free Scarecrows». Members of OPLA killed many civilians and among them the great actor Eleni Papadakis (on April 1943) under the false accusation that she was a girlfriend of appointed by Germans Prime Minister I. Rallis.

The victims of OPLA were many, while the criterion for their choice was political and sometimes incomprehensible. For example, I. Maratos and members of his family were killed in reprisal for transporting Greek officers to Egypt! They even

4. The Liberation of Greece

murdered a young girl who was servant of the family. OPLA's men also killed Minister of Justice C. Ladas on the 1st of May 1948. OPLA was mainly responsible for massive executions in the Feneos area where, on the 16th-18th of July 1944 many «reactionaries» and some collaborators were executed there; 260 people in total, including children. At Feneos they hit the victims with heavy iron (a bell tongue) and stabbed them before they throw them into a natural drain. Kostas Axelos, a noted left intellectual, wrote for all these: «*The Greek communist Party was schizophrenic. On one hand, it struggled for social justice, and on the other, it was OPLA that killed people. The guerrilla war was decent against the conquerors, but not against the compatriots! In December, our Army executed all, Archmarxists, Trotskyists ...In December I realized what mistakes the Party had made...*».

OPLA also dealt with robberies, e.g. the robbery of the Supply Fund and the athletic shoes factory «Alysida». In addition to OPLA, executions of people were carried out by men of the People's Guard, a group like the private police of KKE, and ELAS' Garrison Headquarters who were conducting «small interrogations» of dissidents, who were then usually soon executed. The People's Guards during Occupation functioned only in «free mountainous Greece», while ELAS operated in the occupied and semi-occupied areas. In addition, ELAS was controlled by EAM, while OPLA was ordered exclusively by the KKE. The many «reactive» executions by ELAS and OPLA in December are probably due to a broader plan to exterminate their political opponents, as Yannis Ioannidis, the second man in the KKE hierarchy, had confessed in his memoirs in an interview. The idea was of D. Glynos who proposed it to Ioannidis well before December, «*...to exterminate a few thousand reactionaries in Athens, Piraeus, Thessaloniki, and some other cities*». The rationale of all these actions of the members of the KKE-ELAS-OPLA was that they were possessed by cultivated «class hatred» resulting in killings of innocent people and murders of «reactionary» prisoners.

Varkiza Agreement – Disarmament of ELAS

On the 3rd of January Prime Minister Papandreou resigned, and General N. Plastiras took his place and remained as Prime Minister for the next three months. On the 11th of January, a cease-fire agreement between the Greek government and EAM-ELAS was agreed. Subsequently, on the 12th of February 1945, the Agreement of Varkiza was signed. According to it, ELAS was granted amnesty for political offenses, yet not for unnecessary crimes that had been done on political purposes. Moreover, ELAS was forced into disarmament and consented to the creation of a National Army. The Agreement was signed from ELAS' side by Siantos, Partsalidis, and Tsirimokos. Meanwhile, Archbishop Damaskinos convinced Tsirimokos not to insist on general amnesty as well as on the KKE's involvement in the government. Thereafter, ELAS handed over about half of its weapons. Apparently, ELAS was still aiming for the continuation of the fight on appropriate conditions. Thus, a large number of the weapons that were delivered were the oldest ones. In fact, Tito himself advised ELAS not to hand over all of its weapons. Allied to this, conspirator Ioannidis instructed the communists of ELAS who had hidden weapons to move to Yugoslavia so that they could be safe, and not reveal the hiding spots of their weapons.

Internal communist Conflicts

The united forces of the KKE, EAM, ELAS, the People's Guards, and OPLA were on the opposite side of the Greek government and the British. The KKE was trying to avoid been regarded as leading a rebellion. EAM approved or rejected

4. The Liberation of Greece

suggestions from the Central Committee of ELAS. However, the Socialists Svolos and Tsirimokos had also some influence on the decisions and they were trying to compromise with the government. Yet, a crisis was going on in the KKE due to the accusations against Siantos from the «number two» man of the Party, the powerful Ioannidis, who was saying that Siantos was acting on his initiative and opted in a frontal conflict with the government and the British. The strange thing is that Siantos was characterized as a politician that was favoring the British! Moreover, the KKE's internal conflicts also evolved into contradictory announcements, sometimes favoring the civil war and sometimes declining it. Regarding the Agreement itself, Partsalidis wrote: «*The KKE did not decide on Varkiza's Agreement by itself. It was the communist leader Dimitrov of Bulgaria who handed over the mandate on behalf of Stalin*». However, after the events, Stalin agreed that «*Varkiza was a mistake*» and questioned the authority of Dimitrov.

The Liberation of Thessaloniki

On the 29th of October 1944, all remaining Germans left Thessaloniki. On the 30th of October 1944, the 9th ELAS Division entered the city of Thessaloniki easily, despite Scobie's orders that «*guerrillas should not enter the cities*». It should be noted that G. Modis, who represented the Greek government after the resignation of all EAM' ministers, was placed under restriction at the Mediterranean Hotel. Thus, the leader of EAM in Macedonia, Euripides Bakirtzis, the so-called Red Colonel, and Captain Markos Vafiadis decided wisely that there would be no conflict with the state, in contrast to what would happen in Athens later on December 1944. Three Brigades, mostly Indians of the 4th Indian Division, disembarked in Thessaloniki and were established in the Cape of Great Karabournou. In December, when Siantos ordered Markos Vafiadis to attack the British troops at Thessaloniki, Markos replied that «*at the moment, this is not possible»* because many of his troops left to strike the Phostiridis' guerrillas in Drama and the Anti-communist armed forces in Western Macedonia. In the city of Thessaloniki, arrests were made with the accusation of co-operation with the Germans, as well as individual clashes of opposing groups; most Gendarmerie men were arrested, and some were executed. The communists walked around the city in the evenings, up-roaring slogans in favor of the KKE and against King George. As far as the distribution of the political parties to the city, the leftists prevailed in the highest districts of it, while in the city center and the areas by the sea the anti-communists were the majority.

Markos Vafiadis later accused ELAS' Central Committee of fragmenting his forces and called the Central Committee's officers «*a staff of ordinary soldiers»*. Additionally, T. Makridis who was the chief military brain of ELAS, stated: «*...the retreating Germans had been surrounded in Macedonia and could be exterminated. And the extermination of Germans would give us 40-50 canons, ...yes, we could have captured so many canons, and we could hence have developed accordingly the fighting capacity and strength of our army in Macedonia and ELAS in general. Markos and Bakirtzis though chose to run to Thessaloniki, which they could have taken over at any moment, if they would decide to do so. They abandoned the extermination of the encircled German forces in their region»*.

Fights between Greeks at Kilkis - A bloody masacre

Various armed groups of Anti-communists had been formed in Western and Central Macedonia, especially since mid-1943, that were taking guns and money from Germans to defend themselves against ELAS; PAO had already by then had dissolved. Some former officers of PAO's were in Thessaloniki but they remained mostly unrelated to subsequent events. On

4. The Liberation of Greece

the other hand, the local EDES was very weak and it comprised of only very few members. Moreover, there were aslo some «National Socialists» in Thessaloniki who had taken advantage of the cooperation with Germans, regarding food and black market. The anti-communists mostly joined the Organization of the National Hellenic Army (EES) which was initially a resistance organization but soon took weapons from Germans to face ELAS a few months before the Germans would flee. However, many members of the EES decided to join EDES before confronting ELAS. They then wanted to add a «D» to their hat visor by turning the EES into EDES, but Zervas did not accept them.

As ELAS forces headed to Thessaloniki, the various armed collaborators of the Germans, gendarmes, civil servants and prominent anti-communists followed the opinion of Kyriakos Papadopoulos (Kisa Batzak), who was controlling about 1,500 men. They all went to defend themselves at the town of Kilkis, while the military officers had suggested for all to go in the mountains of Kozani. Fierce battles took then place at Kilkis between ELAS and anti-communists. ELAS men, who were better armored, encircled their opponents, who could not withstand their attack; Subsequently, most of the captured anti-communists were murdered without a trial. In total, the dead anti-communists guerrillas and civilians were over 3,500, therefore the deads of Kilkis of the 4th of November 1944 are considered higher to that of Meligalas.

The change of government in Bulgaria toward communism satisfied ELAS. The same Bulgarian soldiers, who occupied Eastern Macedonia and Thrace, now changed their minds and instead of being monarchists they were transformed to communists! Around the end of November 1944, the Greek government invited Fostiridis to Athens to discuss the situation, and then great forces of ELAS in co-operation with the Bulgarians forced the men of Fostiridis to dissolve. At the same time, Fotistiridis was blocked in Athens and then participated in the fight of Makriyiannis' regimen gendarme camp. The KKE tried to accuse Fostiridis as a partner with the Bulgarian anti-communists. However, this is far from being true! The rivalry between Fostiridis and the Bulgarians was racial. What happened was that the British agent Miller agreed with the new government in Sofia to stop the fights of Bulgarians with Greeks. But this promise was not kept, as ELAS attacked the National Resistance Organizations assisted by Bulgarian Anti-Fascists (communists). Markos Vafiadis wrote for this: «*...by retreating, the Bulgarians handed the cities over to ELAS guerrillas and at the same time gave in ELAS heavy weapons, ammunition, and other supplies. Thus, without personal involvement, they helped ELAS to dismantle the Anton Tsaous (Fostiridis) groups in Eastern Macedonia*». The Bulgarian communists remained in the occupied Hellenic territories until Stalin, following Moscow's «Agreement on zones of influence» ordered the Bulgarian troops to pass into Bulgaria keeping their previous frontiers. It is also impressive that when the Russian General Tolbukhin, reached the pre-war borders of Bulgaria and Greece, he decided to stop there. Stalin's orders were clear: Greece was in the sphere of British influence.

Chapter 5

THE GOVERNMENT INSTABILITY 1944-1947

The period from November 1944 to March 1945 were days of «absolute EAM dominance». After the conqueror's withdrawal, EPON (youth organization of EAM) propagated rapidly while communist leaders were preparing the young men for the events that would follow. The first years after the liberation from the Triple Occupation of the country was a period of great political instability. British Ambassador R. Lepper kept announcing and then denouncing the assigned Prime Ministers. Plastiras disagreed with Lepper saying to him «*I am a friend of the British, but not a slave of the British...and Greece is not a colony*»; however, Lepper did not have the same mindset. Thus, he tried to get rid of «stiff» General Plastiras forcing him to resign after his publication in the right-wing newspaper «Greek blood», of a controversial old letter, where he was calling for an agreement with Italy while the war was still on. At that time, Plastiras had written: «*The terrible regime of the 4th of August not only attempted to declare the war against two overpowering Empires during a time of England's complete weakness, and not only destroyed the Nation, but also attempted to cancel negotiations with Germany to resolve the Italian-Hellenic conflict*».

Immediately, Admiral P. Voulgaris was appointed Prime Minister (from 7/4/1945 to 17/10/1945). From the 17th of October to the 1st of November 1945, due to the inability of the political system to form a government, Archbishop Damaskinos took over the Prime Ministry and on the 30th of December, he became a Regent. Kanelopoulos succeeded Damaskinos as Prime Minister but remained in the cabinet for only 21 days. After that, he resigned under the pressure from the British government that changed opinion on the referendum issue regarding King George, for which proposed a postponement until 1948! From 22/11/1945 to 4/4/1946 Th. Sofoulis was appointed as the Prime Minister, with Kafantaris and Tsouderos as Vice Presidents, while there were non-communist ministers from the resistance personas, such as G. Kartalis of the EKKA, I. Peltekis of Apollon and H. Petmezas of EDES. In December 1945, the government voted for the law on decongesting the prisons. According to this law, three-quarters of the prosecuted prisoners ceased to be in custody. This was a compromising move of Sofoulis favoring the KKE, something like an amnesty. However, many leftists that were released, became the core of the emerging guerrillas of the «third round» of the Civil War that was planned to follow.

Finally, Sofoulis organized fair elections in 1946 and Tsaldaris the leader of the People's Party became the Prime Minister from 18/4/1946 until 24/1/1947. D. Maximos, a former National Bank president, who was Deputy Prime Minister succeeded him from 24/1/1947 to 28/8/1947. Then, Tsaldaris returned as Prime Minister on the 29th of August and stayed only until the 7th of September when he resigned by supporting a government under the aged politician T. Sofoulis. This change in the political scene was an American plan, that aimed for a broader government in Greece representing the civil non-left part of Greeks. It has to be emphasized that during those times Greece had to seek advice from the UK and the USA, even for the most insignificant issues. Moreover, due to the catastrophe of triple occupation, the destroyed villages from the conquerors and the Dekembriana (1944) events, the country's needs for military and financial assistance were huge and therefore the political dependence of Greece on the Anglo-American axis was absolute.

Reconstruction of the National Army and of the Gendarmerie

By the end of 1945, the A' Military Division had been organized under T. Tsakalotos, who had the role to train soldiers. Militia provided the army with appropriate manpower while its men were overseeing social discipline in the country since mid-September of that year. Militia comprised of men from right-wing organizations, former guerrillas, and some leftists. By May 1945, the guards had reached the number of 60,000. However, they acted mostly locally and continued the old vendettas with the communists and old EAM-men. After mid-1945, the government began to appoint men to the Gendarmerie, which was kept only two-thirds of its pre-war manpower due to the losses of Dekembriana. At the end of 1945, the Greek Army included 75,000 men who increased to 120,000 in the following two years. As for the City Police Forces in Athens, Piraeus, Patras, and Corfu, they had also suffered many victims from the communists in the bloody December, and their men had anti-communist feelings.

Since July 1945, a special British mission headed by Sir Charles Wickham aimed to democratize and modernize the Police and Gendarmerie. This mission managed to create peaceful police units but couldn't put an end to the crazy hunt of the left-wingers. The atmosphere, especially in the province, was tensed, and the Gendarmerie had to face the deflections of right-wing and left-wing organizations. The Civil War was emerging, yet not ready to be depicted.

The death of Aris Velouchiotis

Velouchiotis did not participate in Athens' Battles, because he was busy chasing Zervas' men in Epirus. The rebellious Captain of ELAS disagreed with the KKE's leadership, especially for the Varkiza Agreement, so he decided to continue actions in the province against the National Government. Therefore, he asked to meet Zachariadis to present him his views, but he did not receive any response. In June 1945, the KKE considered Velouchiotis as an undisciplined guerrilla and abandoned him, while *Rizospastis* denounced him in public. According to the decision of the 11th plenary session of the Greek communist Party, Thanasis Klaras, (as was the real name of Aris Velouchiotis) was removed from the Party, and then the KKE commanded to its members: «*no bread and no water to Misserias*» (Miserias was the nick-name of Velouchiotis)!

T. Lefterias (a top rank communist) later wrote about the opinion of G. Siantos about A. Velouchiotis: «*Then Siantos tells me: Klaras (Aris Velouchiotis) is an adventurer. He has a lot of weaknesses. Of course, he's one of the seniors in our group, no reason to tell you more details, but he was interfering with us every day here (in Athens), created problems into our organization. So, in order to get rid of him, I told him: leave me and go wherever you wish; just leave Athens. He wanted to go to the mountains in the area of Roumeli to become a guerrilla. I said to him: go to Roumeli, go wherever you want, be a guerrilla, do what you want, just leave Athens*». Thus, Aris went to the area of Roumeli, as the leader of a guerrilla group. However, he exposed by this the Party's scope, since «*our goals regarding guerrilla action is not this, because the purpose of our Party is the development of an armed fight, and not such actions that expose us rather than benefit us in our interactions with the political parties*» (implying the execution of father and son of a Marathea family). It must be noted, that in this period

5. The Government Instability 1944-1947

Velouchiotis, despite having some loyal men, he did not have the level of impact that he used to have. In his movements, he wandered up to Albania, but eventually returned back to his base in Roumeli. The rest of his life reminds us of an ancient tragedy. In June 1945, Velouchiotis was surrounded by national guards around Arta and shot himself in the head, while his friend Tzavellas hugged himself and activated a grenade he had on his chest. Velouchiotis's head became a trophy and a spectacle in villages for several days.

Aris Velouchiotis was adored by a lot of people of EAM-ELAS, but he was very violent and hotheaded. He killed people with his gun, either to punish them for stealing for instance just a hen, or because of insubordination. He personally tortured many and among them the non-left military officer Themis Marinos, who was a Greek captain and Kris Woodhouse his close partner. In August 1942, he ordered the execution of two children, the daughters of John Kordas, who had abandoned ELAS. In July 1942, he kidnaped the 14 years old son of Maratheas, who had been just murdered by ELAS as an «bourgeois» asking for money. Despite the payment he received from the child's mother, (as newspaper Elefthero Vima claimed on the 27th of September 1942) Velouchiotis killed the child and dropped his corpse into a lime kiln. He was also responsible for the slaughter of Meligalas, despite not being present since he instructed the execution of all prisoners. The left Parties approached him as an idol, like Che Guevara. However, after the Varkiza Agreement, the KKE denounced him and it is only far later, at the National Conference of the KKE in 2011, when it was decided to restore his name politically.

White and Red Terrorism

White terrorism is defined as the acts of extra-governmental anti-communists groups who acted against ELAS-KKE. Many white terrorism acts originated from reprisals of non-communists against the atrocities of ELAS. In particular, ELAS at the time of its power entered villages and demanded: a. to be given supplies in the form of clothes, food, and animals; b. volunteers to be classified as fighters; c. those who belonged to organizations other than EAM-ELAS as well as the village reactionaries to surrender. Moreover, ELAS carried out executions of rivals while right after they abducted their properties. If any villagers reacted in some way, they were beaten or even murdered. ELAS' officers used to sign a receipt for the food and animals that had received and were promising compensation after being released from the Germans. This, of course, would have been the case only if it would be by then an EAM-ELAS government. The young men who fled from joining ELAS were put on a blacklist to be killed at the first given opportunity.

In an effort of the non-communists to confront ELAS, various paramilitary groups were formed, and they were acting uncontrollably. They committed several misdemeanors as well and even executed communists for retaliation. According to Article 3 of the Varkiza Agreement, «*the amnesty does not include offenses that were not necessary for achieving a political goal*». After Varkiza, the National Guards, the Police and the gendarmes began searching and arresting communists for crimes committed during Dekembriana and the Occupation. But their men of the state were still not enough, so they decided to seek help from extra-governmental organizations like G. Grivas' organization X. However, after the Varkiza Agreement, this organization was officially disbanded, and its leader planned to participate in politics. Thus, the senior members of X acted in small groups, regardless of leadership. By then, a lot of far-right men were called mistakenly men of X. Moreover, many of the members of Organization X had already been classified as National Guards.

The men of ELAS committed a lot of crimes in Peloponnese, with their leaders A. Velouchiotis, N. Beloyiannis, D. Pirpiris, and A. Blanas, especially from May to October 1944

5. The Government Instability 1944-1947

in Kalamata, Meligalas, Pyrgos, Sparta, and Gargaliani. After the demobilization of ELAS, the anti-communists began to chase the leftists to retaliate. But the sadistic executions of ELAS and OPLA could not be committed by the opposite side to the same extent since they acted having then a government and a State. But the extra-governmental far-right organizations were still in action that had a favorable treatment on behalf of the Gendarmerie. That probably happened mostly because the Gendarmerie had already been through enough fights with ELAS during the Occupation, while communists continuously attacked gendarmes. One of the illegal actions of the far-right organizations was the murder of Kostas Vidalis, who was the editor of the communist newspaper Rizospastis. Besides this one, other small or greater incidents of retaliation took also place, especially in Peloponnese. On the 16th of January 1946, left-wing rebels murdered the leader of Laconia's Organization X, lawyer G. Kontovounisios, his 6-year-old son and their two companions. Two days later, several men, having revolvers and grenades, attacked a left-wing cafe and killed two people. The following day, the funeral of the victims evolved into a rally that resulted in a fight of left-wingers and right-wingers. Police authorities arrested 32 people as suspects for the murderous assault in the cafe. On the 19th of January 1946, about 1,000-armed right-wing extremists led by Vangelis Manganas entered Kalamata to seek revenge for the previous events. They killed eight people, took 50 hostages and they executed six of them. Manganas was not a member of X, but his actions opted for the same anti-communist direction. He continued his terrorist activity and he was eventually arrested. His trial was turbulent, without witnesses, and ended in his acquittal. In October 1948 he became the head of an armed men group in Kalamata and in April 1949 he was arrested again, according to an order given by General Tsakalotos, and was imprisoned. As counter-reactions to the terrorist acts of the far-right groups, the KKE had taken some action at the end of 1945 until 1946; however, these reprisals caused a further increase in the actions of the far-right. Among other events, left-wing politicians I. Pasalidis and N. Grigoriadis were attacked by right-wing paratroopers and were injured.

In general, we can say that in Peloponnese, Roumeli, and Thessaly the far-right prevailed, while in Macedonia the communists had more power. Extreme groups from both sides were responsible for bloody episodes. According to Tsakalotos, from February 1945 until the elections of 1946, there were about 200 groups of armed communists with a force of 10-25 men per group in the countryside. At the same time, more than 80,000 people belonging to EAM and ELAS went through criminal proceedings during 1945. Of course, they were not prosecuted without reason; a lot of things have happened during the two previous «rounds» of civil conflicts. However, state justice showed great rigor when communists were being judged and mildness when anti-com-munists were being judged. Political violence with terrorist attacks had become a daily routine, and from January to May 1946, an average of 68 murders per month was recorded (according to the British police), which were equally divided hunting both groups. Thus, white terrorism was not the only one; it also had coupled with red terrorism.

EVENTS OF 1946

Parliamentary elections of 1946

N. Zachariadis was released from a German concentration camp at Dachau and returned to Greece by a British airplane. However, unlike other hostages from concentration camps, he hadn't lost weight because Germans used him as an interpreter. The KKE found its previous «charismatic» leader and handed over to him the leadership of the Party again. Zachariadis did not have a solid plan of action for the

5. The Government Instability 1944-1947

Communistic Party, but it seemed like he might be flirting with the idea of «third» round of conflicts. Yet, his psychological particular state was obvious. He was absent from the great accomplishments of his party during the triple occupation, the enormous development of EAM and ELAS, and the Dekembriana battle in Athens. He now wanted to gain under his own leadership the Party's success and glory.

In January 1946, the Soviet representative at the UN Headquarters in London, Andrey Vysinsky, denounced «the arbitrary stay of the British forces in Greece and their illegal interference within the country against the democratic citizens». The Greek Foreign Minister Sofianopoulos, (who was left-leaning) did not want to take part in the debate and for this reason he was forced to resign. This appeal of Vyshinsky was successfully disputed by British Foreign Minister Ernest Bevin. Sofoulis decided to go for elections on the 31st of March 1946 by his government. The elections were closely monitored by 1,200 foreign observers, who found them to be smooth with some minor incidences. The KKE decided to abstain from the elections, despite Stalin's instigation through Dimitrof to join a «United Popular Front» with more left-leaning powers as Svolos, Tsirimokos, and others. Overall, two alternatives were available for the KKE: a. the path of democratic procedures with trade union action and people's movement, and b. the path of armed conflict in pursuit of violent seizure of power. An important act that pointed towards the Civil War was the abstention from the elections. Thus, the KKE chose to abstain from the election with the formal excuse-pretext of the so-called «white terrorism».

The decision to abstain was made twenty days prior to elections. Abstention as an action of a rebellious party is like announcing an armed struggle. This is because abstention alone, without the following revolution, is the suicide of the rebellious party. Thirty years ago, after the abstention of the Venizelos' Liberal Party, a coup was followed who led to a separated state of Thessaloniki in 1916. As far as the elections of 1946 are concerned, the people who did not vote were automatically considered suspects for being followers of the KKE and in their personal documents held by the General Security, there was a relevant record: «did not vote in the 1946 elections», hence being suspicious for left-wing opinions! Abstention due to obedience to KKE was estimated by reliable researchers to be about 20-25%, while this percentage also included other small center-left Parties that abstained as well. Thus, KKE followers were far from being the majority. After the elections of 1946, a judge, P. Poulitsas, became the Prime Minister for 4 weeks, until K. Tsaldaris was elected as the leader of the People's Party. Until the next elections of the 5th of March 1950, ten coalition governments were formed. Because of the electoral system, and especially because many parties took part in the first post-war elections, none of the Parties in the Parliament had the absolute majority.

In the summer of 1946, the KKE organized «Groups of Enforced Democratic Fighters» which aimed at passive resistance, and soon at active «mass popular self-defense». Later on, groups of 60-100 men were formed, headed by a Captain and a Commander; they progressively increased their number and them eventually in 1947 formed Headquarters. The responses of Stalin and Tito in the spring of 1946 to the conditions in Greece were pointing towards an armed struggle. However, in autumn of 1946 Stalin was against a massive development of the rebels' armed struggle.

5. The Government Instability 1944-1947

Table 4.
Election results of the 31st of March 1946.
Abstention was about 30-50% but about 25% abstention rate is common in Greek elections.

Parties or United parties	leaders	Votes	%	Seats
United Nationalists		610995	55.12	206
People's Party	Tsaldaris K.			156
Party of Nationalist Liberals	Gonatas S.			38
Trasformation Party	Alexandris A.			5
Penellenic National Party	Sakellariou A.			1
Party of Patriotic Unity	Batsios H.			1
Pro-king party	Lykidis P.			3
Political Group Ahead	Sfaelos D.			1
Labor Greek Party	Dimitratos A.			1
National Political Union		213721	19.28	68
Party of Liberals	Venizelos S.			31
Democratic Socialistic Party	Papandreou G.			27
National Unity Party	Kanellopoulos P.			9
Socialistic Union Greece	KasimatiG.			1
Liberal Party	Sofoulis T.	159525	14.39	48
National Party of Greece	Zervas N.	66027	5.96	20
Unity of Nationalists		32538	2.94	9
Party of Nationalists	Tourkovasilis T.			7
Popular Agricultural Party	Pampoukas G.			2
United Agricultural Parties	Mylonas A.	7447	0.67	1
Independent combinations		12036	1.09	2

International Meeting in Paris

After the end of the war, representatives of many countries gathered in Paris to discuss the establishment of borders, as well as the war compensations that the defeated countries had to pay. The Greek delegation had a large number of diplomats and consultants who did not all have good relations with each other. The head of the delegation was the State Secretary for Foreign Affairs F. Dragoumis. Foreign Minister K. Tsaldaris, the leader of the People's Party, who was also Prime Minister at that time went later to Paris and made a great speech in the Conference, yet he did not manage to influence the decisions; Greece was too small to impose its will. The major aim of Greece was to get war compensation from Germany, Italy, and Bulgaria as well as to acquire Northern Epirus and the Dodecanese. Moreover, Greece called for the borders with Bulgaria to be shaped in such a way so as to provide defensive security against the future aggressive action of the neighboring country, since Bulgaria always aimed for a passage to the Aegean sea. However, at the time, the cold war began to emerge between the two large groups:

a. The Liberal democracies, in which free people can elect his own government among various parties.

b. The Communist states, in which only one Party, participates in the government and would apply the dictatorship of the proletariat. The Soviet Union was a huge country and sought to dominate many East European countries. Essentially, it was its influence that guided, among other countries, Bulgaria, Yugoslavia, and Albania. The Soviets were against Greece's claims, while Americans and the British did not have much power to resist. Finally, Greece succeeded in gaining Dodecanese and only some compensations from Italy; 145 million dollars were given for war reparations, instead of the 6 billion demanded by the Greek delegation.

5. The Government Instability 1944-1947

North Epirus remained in Albanian territory, even though during the war Albania allied with the Nazi forces and participated, yet in a small way, in the attack against Greece. As for the border with Bulgaria, the Russian Foreign Minister Molotov did not accept any negotiations. The British-Americans were slowly changing their attitude and started leaving Greece with no help. Fortunately for Greece, Molotov agreed to give to Greece the Dodecanese, probably from rivalry with Turkey. The internal intricacies during the Occupation and the civil war deprived Greece to be a dominant force after the war. Greece needed help in the form of financial support and armaments to cope with the communistic aggressiveness.

Referendum for the King

In 1946, the Centrist and the left Parties did not accept before elections a referendum for the King's return, despite the promise that Churchill had given to King George. Finally, Sofoulis decided to proclaim the referendum a few months after the elections, which was held on the 1st of September 1946. The KKE participated in the referendum normally. EAM and the KKE worked, as expected, to vote for the republic without a King. Parties of the Centrum, for reasons of principle and tradition, preferred the republic, but they did not campaign for it actively. Gonatas, who was a former Prime Minister and revolutionist in 1922, supported King George. In favor of the King's return were the People's Party and those who had worked with it in the parliamentary elections of the 31st of March 1946. The result of the referendum was «Yes» for the return of King George B' to the throne at a rate of 68.3%.

In areas where communists thought that they were their own, such as Piraeus and Thessaloniki, the results indicated that the votes had been shared. Accusations of fraud followed and, in some way happened. But even without the fraud, the referendum would be in favor of King George, especially after the 1943-1944 actions of the left organizations KKE and EAM-ELAS-OPLA and the bloody December that Athens and other parts of the country had experienced. It was evident that the citizens saw the King as a protector against Communism, and the old division of the bourgeois parties between the Royalists and the Venizelists had been weakened. The non-communists believed the King as the one who would guarantee their democratic regimen against the «dictatorship of the proletariat» that the KKE had attempted to establish through EAM-ELAS'

Chapter 6

THE CIVIL WAR 1946-1949

THE PRELUDE - GUERRILLAS AGAINST THE STATE

Warm-up exercises for the Civil War

As early as 1945, immediately after the Agreement of Varkiza, the public was being prepared for the Civil War with speeches, publications, notices, and funnels (since there were no electric loudspeakers) with accusations against «Monarch-Fascism» and the government. Small groups of guerrillas who did not surrender their weapons were wandering in the mountainous areas, while others were being trained beyond the northern border. There were about 5,000 ELAS guerrillas at Bulkes of Yugoslavia being trained there for the Civil War which was to come. In August 1945 Zachariadis announced the aggressive slogan: «*If necessary, the glorious hymn 'Let's go ELAS, for Greece', will echo again in gorges and mountain peaks*». This invitation had an immediate response. At Christmas in 1945, in the village of Lavara at Didimoticho district, over 200 communists surrounded the Gendarmerie station, they were repelled but there were quite a few victims on both sides.

Increase of the rebel groups throughout Greece

Throughout 1946, small groups of rebels (10-20 people) had attacked various parts of the country, targeting individual gendarmes, Gendarmerie Stations or «reactionaries» according to the KKE terminology. On the 13th of January 1946, after Zachariadis' speech in Volos, there were clashes with the gendarmes and four protesters were killed. In response, the KKE organized a big gathering in the stadium of Panathinaikos. The speaker was the former General Othonaios, who, as he grew older, leaned more to the left. His speech was followed by the events in Peloponnese that have already been mentioned. According to Colonel Tsakalotos, at that time there were about 200 rebel groups throughout Greece, from Peloponnese to Evros. It was a matter of time for conflicts to turn into a bloody Civil War.

Zachariadis decided to start the Civil War during a secret gathering of Executives in the framework of the 2nd Plenary of Central Committee on the 12th-15th of February 1946. Leftist writers highlighted the «White Terrorism» as the reason for KKE's decision to proceed to a Civil War in 1946, which the KKE had prepared a few months earlier on a «self-defense» basis. Then spies, saboteurs, local leaders, dissident traitors, recruits, nurses, food providers, and information networks were organized and contributed greatly to the further development of the guerrillas' war and its support within the various villages. However, all reliable sources argued that the decision about the Civil War had been taken long ago. This may also derive from the very large number of hidden weapons and ammunition that ELAS did not give up. Even large firearms were hidden, which of course were not for self-defense! The self-defense initiative was rather a stage of preparation and development towards the Civil War. EAM had sought to eliminate any other resistance organization until the liberation and for this aim had recruited thousands of men. Both Siantos and Zachariadis had fluctuations in their politics and they were not always hard-core. These fluctuations were related both to the international conjuncture, but also to the wishes of the other communist Parties, particularly from Yugoslavia and the USSR. Bulgarian

6. The Civil War 1946-1949

Dimitrov played the role of the proxy server of opinions. In March 1946, Zachariadis went to Crimea, where Stalin was resting. Stalin agreed to the development of a guerrilla movement and gave Zachariadis instructions, but also, he sent him to Tito for further details. At the end of August 1946, Zachariadis sent a report to Stalin through Dimitroff. Stalin's response arrived on the 11th of November 1946, advising the KKE «*not to focus on the armed fights, but mostly on the political struggle*». It has to be noted that this was a period of international difficulties and the Soviet Union was promoting its state interests elsewhere (there were complications in Czechoslovakia, Poland, and Romania). On the 31st of December 1946, Dimitroff informed the KKE «*not to wait for any other help*». Then, Zachariadis personally addressed «Comrade Stalin» in his letter that ended: «*…we plead you to help us to meet our very serious needs, and we hope soon to receive your decision regarding this matter*». In this letter, Zachariadis asked not only for money but also for material help as he wrote: «*At Varkiza we managed to hide weapons for 20,000 people; unfortunately, due to hasty hiding, most of them fell to the hands of the opponents or broke down; we also need help in clothing, even in food*».

The Civil War is believed to have started on the night of the 30th of March 1946, which was the elections' night, with the assault of a former guerrilla group of ELAS at the Gendarmerie Station of Litochoro, at the district of Katerini, although this was probably a kind of prelude to the drama. Captain Ypsilantis (Alexis Rosios), was in charge of the attack with 60 men who used incendiary grenades as well. Some gendarmes were killed before they even got out of their beds. However, the battle lasted a few hours. Early in the morning, the guerrilla group fled to Mount Olympus. Twelve people (gendarmes or National guards) were killed by this attack, while the Gendarmerie Station was burned. Interestingly, in the wider area of Litochoro episodes between right-wing and left-wing partisans had not occurred until then. Litochoro's Gendarmerie Station was just a rehearsal for what would follow. Apparently, it seemed to KKE a convenient target at the time.

On the 16th of June 1946, an evolving movement of the KKE in the army dismantled at the last minute with some arrests based on the Divisions of Larisa, Trikala, and Kozani. On the 18th of June, the Greek Parliament adopted the Third Resolution on «Emergency Measures in the Public Order and Security». According to this, the death penalty was imposed on anyone who wanted the assignment of Greek territory to a foreign state. The Police became entitled to capture and interrogate suspects for days without trial, as well as to displace, and to prohibit strikes as well as movements beyond a certain time. Generally, the measures that were voted abolished the principle of Democracy, but they were then deemed necessary due to the tense situation. The KKE newspaper Rizospastis criticized the Third Resolution severely and KKE organized a general strike as a protest, yet with minimum participation; this was because the majority was not supporting the KKE any more, while EAM had already faded.

On the 30th of June, left men attacked Naoussa unsuccessfully and retreated after a two-hour battle with sections of the NA and the gendarmes. On the 5th of July 1946 Pontocerassia, a district of Kilkis, was attacked by guerrillas and there were 7 dead, 33 injured, and 40 deserters. The reaction of the state was immediate and effective. The deserters were captured and tried by a military court and executed. In July 1946, Zachariadis ordered Markos Vafiadis to organize all the armed men who were already on the mountains. In the meantime, the government had displaced the most dangerous of ELAS' officers in the islands. This action opened the way for KKE's party leaders to become Colonels, Brigadiers, and Generals of the guerrilla's army in the Civil War. In July and August 1946, many assailants attacked Gendarmerie Stations with varying outcomes, resulting in many

6. The Civil War 1946-1949

victims, dead or injured, as well as some who were taken as prisoners. On 14th of September 1946, an attack was made to the Police Station of Pirsogianni, a village near Konitsa. The gendarmes were defending themselves for hours, but in the end, they were all killed.

From the 16th of September 1946, the General Staff of the Greek State assigned the military to assume the security of the country, because the extent of the conflict with the rebels that was perceived it would follow. At the same time, the Gendarmerie organized the first «hunting missions», which were done with flexible groups of 60-80 men suitable for guerrilla warfare. These movements broke down when the army was better organized. On the 24th of September 1946, the 1,500 rebels attacked the town of Deskati of Grevena district, where the battle lasted more than 12 hours. The defenders broke the fire barrier with difficulty and hence escaped from captivity and execution. There were 47 dead of the defenders and among them two officers. On the evening of the 30th of September 1946, a rebel attack took place in Naoussa, with temporary success. The guerrillas burned homes of dissidents and committed a few murders, but they left at dawn after hard fighting. At the beginning of November 1946, Markos Vafiadis announced the creation of the General Headquarters of the guerrillas. On the 13th of November 1946, many rebels from Yugoslavia crossed the Greek borders and about 300 of them invaded the city of Skra. They attacked and neutralized the reaction of 60 men of the NA. Additionally, they murdered two Mayors and a brave woman, the school-teacher Vasiliki Papathanasiou. In November 1946, there have been in total 41 attacks by the rebels and clashes with sections of the NA and the Gendarmerie throughout Macedonia, Thrace, and Thessaly. On the other hand, several actions were undertaken by the NA in 1946 to confront guerrillas, yet with poor results because guerrillas were constantly changing positions and had avoided fighting when the attackers were numerous. On Christmas Day of 1946 such an attack took place at Fitia, a village at Vermion mountain. For this attack, the C division of the Greek Army stated: *«... the communist-gang attacked the village and they robbed about 40 houses in which eleven elderly people and children were burned alive»*. This fact impressed the public opinion but also provoked an aggravation of retaliation from the other side.

OPLA's terrorism in Thessaloniki during 1946-1947

The forces of OPLA after the Occupation had an important role in Thessaloniki, with attacks on gendarmes, kiosks, individuals, cafes and military personnel. On the 30th of April 1947, early in the morning, OPLA attempted a serious attack on Aviation officers. Two grenades were thrown onto an aviation military bus, resulting in two dead and six injured men. OPLA was neutralized after the arrest of one of the perpetrators. On the 28th of August 1947, the trial of 67 accused rebels resulted in 52 death sentences and 7 life sentences as well as 8 acquittals.

The rival armies in the Civil War

In the Civil War, the National Army of the Greek State (NA) opposed the left guerrillas, which called themselves as Democratic Army of Greece (DA). Of course, this name is misleading as no army can be democratic! The general secretary of the KKE Nikos Zachariadis was influencing military decisions. He accomplished his communistic studies in the USSR and was a Soviet citizen. However, Zachariadis did not have military knowledge, and therefore DA's Chief-commander was most of the time Markos Vafiadis, a former prominent Captain of ELAS. The generals of DA were Kikitsas, Goussias, Karayiorgis, and Vladas. Out of these, only Kikitsas was a former military officer and participated as the «general organizer of the DA's General Headquarters». The other three Generals were

6. The Civil War 1946-1949

high-ranking members of the communist Party and hence they became Generals having this qualification. Generals Sarafis, Bakirtzis, Mandakas, and Colonel Makridis were eventually displaced by the state's decisions on islands (exiles) and hence did not participate in the Civil War. The arrangement of the DA was initially characterized by various local strategies, but finally, when the guerrilla army was confined to the mountains of Western Macedonia and Epirus, there was a General Headquarter and eleven Divisions just like the organization of the Greek National Army. The DA soldiers and low-rank officers were villagers, mostly farmers. The working class of the cities did not replenish much the staff of the DA, except of a few high-ranking KKE's Executives who were formerly workers but turned out to be paid as KKE employees. Zachariadis often encouraged urban workers to be classified in the DA; he also changed the enlighteners, yet with weak effectiveness. Several former military officers, who had previously joined ELAS, also participated in the DA. Rebels also used women as soldiers beyond auxiliary work they were employed, i.e. cooks, drivers, nurses, etc. In general, many men and women in the countryside had been forced compulsorily to be recruited in DA.

Zachariadis worked to stop the lack of professional Executives of the DA by operating in the mountains a «School of Officers» of the General Staff, which were attended by men and women who were distinguished in their units. A total of 2,750 men graduated as lieutenants from this School, with its initial graduates participating in the battles of 1947. As far as the Greek National Army was concerned, this was still under reconstruction at the beginning of the Civil War. There were gendarmes and military units among the rookies that the state was trying to train. Spiliotopoulos was appointed as the Chief General of the army. He had taken over the command of Athens even before the departure of Germans. He was a skillful man, fair, and objective, so he chose the best officers to manage the new Units by avoiding any party interventions. He even sent his son to fight on the front, where he was finally killed. However, the assembled units had reduced manpower and had many other voids, i.e. they did not have enough machine guns.

Since the first fights with the rebels, it was obvious that the NA had weaker weaponry and limited information network. Moreover, another hazard for the NA was the fact that many leftists were enlisted in the Gendarmerie, and hence they left in some conflicts, or they abruptly changed side during the fighting. To overcome the lack of forces and information useful for the NA, it was decided to form armed groups called MEA (National Security Units), MAY (Rural Defense Units) and later established the TEA (Ethnic Guard Defense). Progressively, many of the existing National Guard administrations had transformed into corresponding regular army formations.

The armament of «Democratic Army»

In addition to weapons that had not been delivered after the Varkiza Agreement, the guerrillas continued to receive weapons and supplies from Eastern European countries, where communist regimes existed such as Yugoslavia, Poland, Czechoslovakia, Hungary, and Romania. The armament was transported in all ways, i.e. by road, in part by air, but also by ships arriving in the ports of Albania, usually in Durres. The ships were mainly Polish (at least 10 missions have been recorded). Yugoslavia, which was the closest country, gave most of the DA support. In 1949, 30 DA men were trained as pilots, and 15 planes were ready to be sent, but they could not operate because of the lack of an airport.

The great degree of support to guerrillas by materials, albeit with the small number of armed men who came from the USSR «satellite countries» (i.e. men from South Yugoslavia, Albania and Bulgaria), led many military persons or respective

6. The Civil War 1946-1949

statements to refer for this period, not to a Civil War, but to a «foreign origin rebellion» using the terms «gangsters», «EAM-Bulgars» and «gang warfare». In general, a very small number of rebels came from Bulgaria, and about 150 Tsams from Albania were recruited. Sometimes Albanians or guerrillas from the Albanian territory bombed Greek sections from their own border side. However, it is obvious that in the battles Greeks fought with Greeks (even brother with brother) and therefore the term «Civil War» is considered as the most realistic term. Certainly, both sides of the war had great help from their allies.

Stalin had many fluctuations in his mind concerning the support and had hesitations of expanding the war, depending on respective developments in international affairs. He wanted to have a hot spot in Greece, but he did not dare to go further until the absolute dominance of the KKE. Thus, sometimes he encouraged, while other times suspended the Civil War for «Svarnut» (which means folding the carpet).

The armament of the National Army

The NA was armored by the United Kingdom until the February 1947 when the British government announced that it would stop all aid to Greece due to its financial weakness. But Harry Truman, the US President, announced on the 12th of March 1947 that his country would financially and militarily support Greece. The US Assistance Mechanism (General Marshall's Plan) was soon activated, and hence the USA provided a lot of money to rebuild the country, as well as the NA. However, US modern arms deliveries delayed reaching Greece, and when they finally arrived «the verdict was nearly announced», in the sense that the DA was territorially restricted and had back up troubles. The military aircrafts were used for reconnaissance flights as well as for attacking the guerrillas and hence played a major role in the outcome of the battles.

The form of the war

In the beginning, the Civil War was a classic guerrilla war and it was characterized by abrupt attacks and continuous movements of guerrillas who avoided the clashes, but they suddenly were strucking whenever they would find the defensive gendarmes or the NA in a weak position. Thus, in the first two years of the Civil War, the guerrillas had major successes and the NA had problems of adjustment to the guerrilla way of war.

EVENTS OF 1947

In January 1947, an international UN's Search Committee received testimonies in Athens and Thessaloniki. Representatives of the Soviet Union and Poland met Markos Vafiadis. The Committee went afterward to Bulkes and Belgrade to meet other communists. At the end of May 1947, the Committee submitted to the UN Security Council a statement, concluding that the war in Greece was prompted by other countries and supported mainly by Albania, Yugoslavia, and Bulgaria, as it was obviously the case.

In early February 1947, Captain Spiliotopoulos speaking in a meeting of the State and Military leadership predicted that the Civil war would last at least three more years. Politicians were disturbed by these words and they placed Spiliotopoulos in the inactive position of Army Inspector. General K. Ventiris was then appointed as the new leader of the NA. Subsequently, the Minister of Public Security N. Zervas took action in Peloponnese, where small groups of rebels constantly were attacking Gendarmerie Stations killing gendarmes, while extreme-right groups made reprisals by killing communists. On the 15th of February 1947, the communist guerrillas attacked

6. The Civil War 1946-1949

Sparta, surrendered the Gendarmerie and released 230 inmates from prison. Several of them were political prisoners; 140 escaped prisoners who followed the rebels. On the 21st of March 1947, guerrillas trapped and killed Captain Katsareas in Peloponnese, along with other four men. After this event, the far-right extremists invaded a concentration camp at Gythion and murdered many communists. The newspaper Rizospastis quoted for this that about 31 men were dead from this action while dozens were injured. In the same evening, the right extremists invaded the offices of the Gythion Gendarmerie and kidnapped eight prisoners from the detention facility and killed them. The government forced to declare military law in Southern Peloponnese and Zervas ordered the arrest of about 500 members of EAM. He also gave orders and thereafter put into prison far-right paratroopers and men of the late Organization X. Thus, Peloponnese would be for a while calm but this would not last for long.

On the 20th of March 1947, the high-rank communist I. Zevgos was assassinated by many shots in a central street in Thessaloniki. A few days before his assassination he had published an article entitled «*no more blood*», that was seeking compromise. The murderer, named C. Vlachos, was arrested immediately and he proved to be a communist who had just returned from the notorious Bullkes of Yugoslavia. The newspapers considered the killing as a Communistic provocation. Later, Markos Vafiadis wrote that he considered Zachariadis as the moral perpetrator of this assassination! Rizospastis accused the right-wing men and the Minister of Public Security N. Zervas himself as the instigators. Vlahos was later hospitalized in a psychiatric hospital on the island of Leros.

On the 12th of March, US President Harry Truman announced his decision on economic and military support Greece and Turkey. In the spring of 1947, many attacks were made, followed by atrocities of communists in many villages across the Greek territory. In the village of Velvendos, public buildings and many houses were burned, where six women were also burned. Many priests were murdered in Grevena. It is impossible to mention these attacks in detail because they were truly numerous. On the 22nd of April Zachariadis sent a letter of briefing to Tito with a plan to establish a regular guerrilla army.

On the 1st of April, King George suddenly died at the age of 57 from a heart attack and his brother Paul immediately succeeded him. King George was an unlucky King, divorced, inward, and melancholic. In his last year, he was the King of a country that was disturbed by a bloody and devastating Civil War.

On the 6th of April, Zachariadis met Ioannidis in Belgrade while the campaign of the «Terminus» operation was happening, and the National Army men climbed up the mountains to search for guerrillas. The heavy cold and the snow did not allow the NA to surprise the rival forces and hence it did not achieve the plan of encircling and capturing the rebels. On the 20th of May, the former leader of the KKE G. Siantos, died at the age of 67 from heart disease as was inpatient at the private medical Department, headed by Professor P. Kokkalis. Siantos had argued before dying that reconciliation should be sought for peace. In May, operation «IERAX» was launched, where the Second Division of NA isolated the guerrillas who were in Hassia and Antichassia mountains and thus weakened the forces of Thessaly Headquarters. cutting off their capability to escape to Grammos. In the same summer, the operations of «STORK» and «KYKNOS» took place in Kissavos, Pelion and the mountains Kaimaktsalan, Vermio, Olympus and Othri with no success, because the rebels moved northerly without engaging in serious battles.

The KORACS (KROAK) operation was followed by an attack on the Grammos, but Markos left only four battalions in Grammos, and with the bulk of his men moved to Ioannina by occupying the bridge at Bourazani in the Aoos River and the surrounding hills. Ioannina was then in danger, where there

6. The Civil War 1946-1949

were only 400 men of the NA. Several sections of the DA passed through Albania, and there were rumors that Albania was attacking Greece. The guerrillas hesitated to proceed to Ioannina and opted for the small town of Grevena. On the 27th of June, Porphyrogenis, as a spokesman for the KKE and the DA, in his speech to a conference of the Communistic Party of France, said that «*the KKE would form a separate State government in Northern Greece*». Then Zervas ordered precautionary arrests throughout the country and hence between 9th and 10th of July approximately 4,000 communists were captured and displaced in the islands Ikaria and Jura. On the evening of 24th of July, the 4,000 men of DA headed by G. Giannoulis attacked unsuccessfully Grevena, because the experienced Lieutenant Colonel K. Pantazis counterattacked and the guerrillas retreated.

Throughout the summer and September, the NA continued to operate under the name «VELOS» in the mountains of Grammos, Smolika, and Vitsi, yet without spectacular results. From the 19th of September to the 12th of October with the operation «LAILAPS», they attacked the forces of the «General» Goussias of the DA in Roumeli. Meanwhile, on the 23rd of September 1947, Goussias moved with his men from Agrafa to Northern Pindos with Captain Giotis (pseudonym of Charalampos Florakis, the later MP and Secretary-General of the KKE). A large group of 4,500 people, (guerrillas and 1,300 unarmed women and children), was formed to cross cold and snowy mountain pathways for 15 days; many victims were left behind due to exhaustion, freezing, and frostbites. Most of the civilians were either violently recruited or they spontaneously followed the rebels being close relatives to them. On the 5th of September, Markos submitted to the UN General Assembly a memorandum in which he stated that he believes in a parliamentary democracy while seeking truce, reconciliation, and a government of National Unity from all Parties. At the same time, Prime Minister T. Sofoulis, who had previously announced an amnesty to those rebels that surrendered (4,000 people were surrendered), extended the duration of the amnesty for another two months, yet with no further result. On the 10th of September 1947, a Markos Vafiadis's letter was published at the London Times (Zachariadis was disturbed by Markos's publicity) and stated that *«we are not servants of the Slavs»*. On the 11th of September, Zachariadis with 6 of the 25 members of the Central Committee of the KKE decided to try to form a government in «Free Greece». With this decision, he probably disagreed with EAM. At the 3rd Plenary session of the Greek communist Party on the 12th-15th of September the operational plan of the KKE with the codenamed «Limnes» was presented and approved. This prompted the occupation of a large region of Thessaly and Macedonia, via control of the main roadways from Thessaly to Ioannina, Kozani and Katerini and the very ambitious occupation of Thessaloniki.

The necessary conditions for the implementation of the «Lakes» project were to reinforce the DA with anti-aircraft guns, the navy with small fast crafts, marine mines, aviation, and to recruit a further 20,000 men (the most difficult) to have a total of 60,000 men by spring 1948. On the 17th of October 1947 provisions of the Third Resolution on **«Emergency Measures in the Public Order and Security»** were supplemented and the circulation of the newspapers Rizospastis and Free Greece, which was edited although the Civil War was in progress, was banned. On the night of the 18th of October ten battalions of guerrillas surrounded Metsovo and managed to enter the village killing those who thought they were «Reactionists» and burned the local school and the Gendarmerie Station. The Mayor of Metsovo, Vasilis Zaousis, committed suicide in order not to be arrested by the guerrillas. Major Paladas two days later attacked and expelled the guerrillas from the village. The attack on Metsovo served as undercover for drawing the attention out of the phalanx led by Goussias, which meanwhile reached Vovousa. At the end of November 1947, Captain Ypsilantis

6. The Civil War 1946-1949

attacked Delvinaki, where he freed 40 communists and he finally reached the Murgana Mountains. There was violent recruitment of young men and girls on his excursions. Gatzogiannis described in his book «Helen» that about 80 girls were recruited violently in the village of Lia, including his 15 years old sister. At that time, with the help of KKE's illegal mechanism, A. Hatzis, A. Tzimas, and D. Partsalidis escaped from the island of Ikaria.

A Provisional Democratic Government in the mountains

On the 23rd of December 1947, the so-called «Provisional Democratic government» (PDG) of the KKE was formed in the mountain with rhe following administration: Prime Minister and Minister of the Military: M. Vafiadis; Vice President and Minister of the Interior: I. Ioannidis; Minister of Foreign Affairs: P. Roussos; Minister of Health & Welfare and Minister of Provisional Education: P. Kokkalis; Minister of Finance: F. Bartziotas; Minister of National Economy: L. Strigos; Minister of Agriculture: D. Vladas; Minister of Justice: M. Porphyrogenis. However, not any country recognized the provisional government from the KKE, despite the military help that the Soviet bloc countries were sending to the DA. It is worth saying for this period that the USA had used already an atomic bomb in Japan and the USSR was not ready for general military conflict.

The attack to Konitsa

In December 1947 Zachariadis had in his mind the small town of Konitsa, which is very close to the border with Albania and it had many defensive disadvantages. On Christmas Eve, several soldiers and officers serving in Konitsa had been on leave. On the 25th of December 1947, at the dawn of Christmas, the DA hit the Bourazanis bridge and immediately launched the attack to Konitsa. On the first day of the battle, Colonel Dovas was injured when his jeep passed over a mine. The general administration of Konitsa was immediately overtaken by Major Paladas. The Dakota airplanes had been deployed for the NA, while fighter planes also attacked the guerrilla's positions. Then the communists made a strategic mistake; they preferred to enter the city early without checking the hills. Thus, the 200 men were neutralized. The NA hence took on the significant strategic position of the neighboring hills. When the Battalion of Lygerakis reached Konitsa, the guerrillas of the DA left the fights after the 6th of January 1948. During that attack, there had been many losses on both sides, but most of the DA. Zachariadis received later on strong criticism of his swift choice to attack Konitsa. Markos also accepted criticism and he stated that the seizure of cities proved to be impossible and bloody. The next day of the last battle, Queen Frederica went to Konitsa alone (King Paul was ill) and spoke to soldiers in order to stimulate the morale of the defenders.

Immediately after the attack on Konitsa, the whims and criticisms of the winners' camp began. The military Commander Ventiris submitted his resignation and General Giantzis was promoted to fill his post. Moreover, in 1947 the guerrillas had made numerous damages to railways and public utilities, as well as they executed many attacks to other towns and cities like Kalavryta, Amaliada, Giannitsa, Edessa, Florina, Grevena, Metsovo, and Atalanti. Furthermore, immediately after the attack in Konitsa, there were massive arrests of communists in Attica by policemen. EAM-and the KKE and their various affiliated organizations were outlawed, and the official state was showing its strength.

Migration of villagers to the cities

In mid-1947 a wave of migration from the villages to cities

began. This was made in part due to the fear of the guerrillas, but also by the orders of the NA. The desertion of the villages deprived the DA of its previous convenience to getting supplies from them; also, the cities were priming with villagers who hated the guerrillas. Subsequently, problems with housing, food, hygiene, and work offers were created

EVENTS OF 1948

On the 6th of January 1948, the Sofoulis government voted in Parliament the 509 State Security Measures and outlawed the KKE and EAM. With this decision the state showed its strength, but it inevitably ceased to be a «pure democracy». This decision potentiated the dynamic of the Minister of Public Order. On the 9th and 10th of February, the guerrillas carried a cannon in the 8th km outside of Thessaloniki and bombed the city. About 40 gun fires were shot and there were six dead and seven injured. The C Division of the NA quickly moved and within three days arrested 141 guerrillas, while 158 guerrillas were dead. The arrestees were tried by a military court which sentenced to death 52 people, while there were 15 severe sentences and 44 acquittals. On the 24th of February, the American General Alward Van Fleet arrived in Greece as the Head of the US military mission and thus the British General Rowgling (who thought that the rebels could be beaten by a regular army) stopped to intervene. It was then decided that the British would continue to train the army, while the Americans would take care of the supplies and would advise on tactics. Van Fleet was a strong personality with a lot of military experience and imposed his opinion on all matters of military leadership. Moreover, he had cultivated good relationships with King Paul and Queen Frederica who was taking many initiatives; among others, she was communicating informally with the American General George Marshall.

Operation STORK

The Murgana mountain range begins in Albania and expands over to Greece. The DA dominated it from November 1947 and threatened the 8th neighboring Division of NA. At the end of February and March 1948, two unsuccessful attempts were made by the NA to expel the guerrillas from the Murgana heights. Thus, Murgana continued to be under the control of the guerrillas until the end of August 1947. It must be noted that in 1971, 120 skeletons of soldiers of the NA were discovered in a mass grave with their hands tied with cables, indicating that guerrillas executed prisoners.

In April and May 1948, the «CHARAVGI» (Dawn) project was planned in Middle Greece, with an Army Corps under Tsakalotos. The Commander gave in advance orders to arrest 4,500 leftists who were accused of reinvigorating the DA. All the arrested men were banished or imprisoned. Since the guerrillas ceased to be supported by the peasants, the action of the NA was easy and hence the guerrillas vanished in the area between Lamia and Athens; 2,500 of the communists were killed, and about 2,000 people captured. Tsakalotos sought to take this initiative, which proved to be efficient. But the leader of guerrillas, Captain Diamantis, managed to escape to Agrafa. As soon as Tsakalotos cleansed the area of Roumeli from the rebels, he gathered many forces against the Murgana mountain range and launched an attack on the 28th of August. The battles lasted for 18 days when the DA retreated to Zagoria. Several guerrillas and wounded men managed to retreat to Albania.

Events in the prisons of Sparta

On the 14th of April, after the death of Gendarmerie Colonel Panagiotopoulos and his four men from a mine, many of his

6. The Civil War 1946-1949

gendarmes invaded Sparta's prison and killed 26 prisoners, as well as Commander-in-chief Major Fitsios, who tried to halt them. It seems that the state had been dismantled. It should be noted that in Sparta during 1944-1945, many gendarmes, army assailants, and citizens were imprisoned with ELAS initiatives, while many of them were murdered. In conclusion, the «vendetta» was evolving!

The Murder of Minister C. Ladas

On the 1st of May, a man dressed as a sergeant murdered Minister Christos Ladas and a policeman by a grenade. A few hours after Ladas' murder, the government declared a military law, but also executed 88 guerrillas who had long been before sentenced to death. The perpetrator of the murder of the minister was arrested but escaped the death sentence because he disclosed classified information.

The Murder of George Polk

On the 16th of May, the American journalist George Polk was found floating on the Thermaikos Gulf of Thessaloniki with a bullet in his skull. As it was known, Polk sought to meet Commander-in-Chief Markos Vafiadis for an interview. Polk had spent enough time in Greece, and he had married a Greek flight attendant. From Polk's talks, he seemed to like the guerrillas and he mentioned that he had received threatening phone calls. The investigation of the assassination was then taken by the Vice Director of the Thessaloniki Security Section, Major N. Mouschountis. Finally, after three months of investigations and interrogation, two communists, A. Mouzenidis and E. Vasvanas, were accused as the perpetrators; G. Staktopoulos was accused as the moral perpetrator. The mother of Staktopoulos was among the accused ones, as she was blamed for writing in an envelope the address, with which Polk's whereabouts were sent to the 3rd

Police Department of Thessaloniki. Mr. Staktopoulos' mother had admitted that she had written this address, but she was acquitted in the trial, although there were positive yet problematic statements from her by two reputable graphologists from Athens. The investigations and the subsequent trial were attended by USA's General William Donovan, as the spokesperson for the League of American Associates and Journalists; however, he was, in fact, a senior USA Intelligence officer. The natural perpetrators were not at the trial, but only Staktopoulos, who admitted, but later denied the charges.

Court decided for Staktopoulos life sentences in jail, while the two perpetrators were sentenced to death. The official state view was that the Cominform had planned the murder to expose Greece to international public opinion. However, when Staktopoulos was released in 1960, he continued for years to refuse his involvement in the murder.

Several books and cinema movies were produced for the Polk case. However, the murder of that American journalist is still a dark issue. Theoretically, the supporting versions were: that Polk was killed: a. by communists as a provocation, b. by a partisan far-right organization, c. by a foreign agent, English or American, and d. by a paid murderer with K. Tsaldaris as the instigator. The answers are pending! Interestingly, in a book by the communist Captain Mavros (N. Hatzinikolaou), published in 2008, it was written that the communist Vasvanas was Polk's murderer.

The CORONIS Plan for an attack on mountain Grammos

At the beginning of May 1948, the CORONIS plan was given to large division administrations, but it had structural disadvantages. In the north of Pindos, from the 13th of March to the 20th of August 1948, the DA constructed 7,200 pillboxes, 500 howitzers, and 150 km entrenched with a total length of

6. The Civil War 1946-1949

approximately 150 km. The NA had to move in two opposite directions across the border to encroach the strengths of the DA. Tsakalotos was invited to Epirus one month later, and on the 1st of August after six days of effort, the significant ridge of Mount Kleftis was dominated. Thereafter, many smaller mountains were conquered by the NA. On the 14th of August, the 9th Division of the DA dissolved the 102nd Brigade of DA in the area of Batras. On the 16th of August Aetomilitsa was captured. Progressively, the positions of the DA were unsecured and there was a risk of surrounding it. On the 21st of August, a successful maneuver was done, with which the DA army transported from Grammos to Vitsi. Two routes were used for this purpose: one safe through Albania and one dangerous through the NA lines. The B' Division of NA was moved later to attack the DA on Vitsi; however, the volume of the DA from Grammos moved securely to Vitsi, giving to guerrillas the opportunity to rest and organize their defense. Two other DA brigades from Central and Eastern Macedonia, as well as about 1,000 men from Bullkes of Yugoslavia, gathered in Vitsi.

In September 1948, the NA with the B' Division failed to defeat the guerrilla forces in Mali Madi and it had many losses. Despite the fighters of the B' Army Corps did not expect to encounter severe resistance, on the 9th and 10th of September the guerrillas attacked and caused an unexpected panic and dissolution of the NA units. Soon the area of Kastoria was filled with fugitives of the NA, many of them drunk. On the 13th of September the DA captured the rocky ridge of Rampatin and other mountains of Kastoria. A serious crisis then came upon the Headquarters of the NA leadership at Vitsi. Many senior officers accused General Kitrilaki as well as the Brigadier and the staff of the 22nd Brigade as insufficient. At that time, the leadership of the NA and the discipline was in confusion. Thus, several people were ordered and sent to the military court for desertion, while the disbanded units were quickly rebuilt, and the discipline restored. On the 19th of September, the DA attacked the NA around Kastoria but faced a stunning resistance and eventually lost the ground that was won a few days prior. In that battle, the NA had aircrafts for reconnaissance flights and for attacking the guerrillas with bombs, rockets, and machine guns.

The DA retreated in its secure quarters in mountains having many losses that would be difficult to replenish. There, 528 guerrillas were counted as dead and many more as injured. Prime Minister T. Sofoulis went to Kastoria on the 21st of September, despite his advanced age, so as to stimulate the morale of the army and people. Those difficult days for the NA, Tsakalotos had just recovered from gastrointestinal bleeding and he was called suddenly to take over A' and B' Army Corps. This brilliant General then called for a full independence movement from Mount Vermio to the Adriatic, he took over the crushed in B' Army Corps and replaced its failed officers with his own. He also merged to it the soldiers of General Manidakis (who was co-fighting with him at Rimini), despite the reactions of Yantzi and Van Fleet. A flavor of victory was redistributed to the NA and, after some other operations of the B' Army Corps, the occupation of heights around Kastoria was secured. The situation in Vitsi was then more stable and because of the winter, military works went in halt. General Kalogeropoulos returned in command of the B' Army Corps and Tsakalotos was stopped from the responsibility of the Grammos-Vitsi region.

The Political instability of 1948

S. Venizelos in early November 1948 announced that the 54 Liberal MPs withdrew their support to the government. Sofoulis immediately resigned and formed a new government on the 18th of November, with the same format of a coalition between the People's Party and those of his Liberals who remained loyal to him. However, he managed to be voted from the Parliament by a single vote majority as he was supported by Spyros

Markezinis, the leader of a small Party. On the 25th of November, the Prime Minister suffered a severe heart attack but managed to survive as he was hospitalized in his office and soon recovered.

The Race in Peloponnese – the DOVE (Peristera) operation

After settling the situation on the front towards Vitsi, in early December 1948, Tsakalotos with the A' Army Corp was ordered to fight the guerrillas in Peloponnese; he started by taking his team, the Manidakis Division and three units of Specific Forces. In Peloponnese the situation was problematic because, after the violence of ELAS, the right-wing paramilitaries had been fighting the guerrillas, while many new ones appeared in the mountains, as they took a movement initiative gathering their strength. Since January 1948, the uncompromising communist leader Stefanos Giouzelis had been sent as the Chief leader in Peloponnese. There, he ruled with great rigidity and discipline, following Aris Velouchiotis's methods. He also managed to increase to 3,000, the 800 men he found at the beginning of his leadership.

The open country of Peloponnese was for months in the authority of the communist guerrillas, while the NA and the Gendarmerie controlled the cities and they were expecting attacks. However, on the 30th of August the DA failed to occupy Dimitsana after a brave resistance for 10 hours of 320 defenders, gendarmes, and armed citizens. The guerrillas run off, leaving 117 dead on the battlefield. This battle was the beginning of further victories of the NA in Peloponnese. When Tsakalotos was ready to fight guerrillas according to «DOVE operation», he began with 4,500 preventive arrests of communists or suspects for helping guerrillas at villages and towns. Then he repeated the tactic that had been implemented in Roumeli the previous year. The arrested were immediately transferred to Makronisos and Trikeri. This operation caused great pressure for Giouzelis' guerrillas. The actual battle for Peloponnese (in fact many small battles) started on the 3rd of January 1949 and ended on the 30th of the same month with the complete crush of Giouzelis' guerrillas; it could not had happened differently. More than 40,000 men of the NA would defeat the 3,500 leftist guerrillas. The biggest battle took place in Leonidion, where a guerrilla attack was repelled. The men of the NA neutralized the DA men at the Agios Vasilios, leaving 180 of them dead. In the next few months, a few small guerrilla groups ended up dying in the mountains from hunger and exhaustion. It was due that the previously frightened villagers had been encouraged and stopped helping the rebels. Giouzelis fled but he was eventually killed outside Peloponnese in September 1949.

Disagreement of Vafiadis with Zachariadis

On the 28th of June 1948, the expulsion of Yugoslavia from Cominform was announced in Moscow. This was because Stalin did not tolerate Tito's independence of opinion and foreign policy. Thereafter, Tito's secret contacts with Americans took place. Tito was asking the USA for financial support in such a subtle manner so as not to be characterized as an enemy of the USSR. The Americans in return were asking to cease supporting the DA. Immediately after the announcement of Tito's break with Stalin, serious dilemmas raised among the top Executives of the DA and the KKE about this practice. Markos Vafiadis wanted no action of the KKE against Tito, because he had great hope on Tito's help. Therefore, he disagreed with Zachariadis who was 100% with Stalin and he had a different opinion on the tactic for the war. Markos was soon quashed by the leadership of the DA for «psychological problems», and he

6. The Civil War 1946-1949

was sent to be hospitalized in Moscow. He stayed there for three months but did not change his mind. In March 1949 Ioannidis was appointed as Markos' Deputy, and D. Partsalidis[5], as the Prime Minister of the mountain government. Three Slavophones with Bulgarian consciousness participated in the new government: Pascal Mitrovski, Stavro Gochev, and Vangelis Kotsiev. The acquisition of Greece's northern region, Macedonia, was their ultimate aim.

In November 1948, Markos returned from Moscow and suggested a memorandum (a «platform» as he said), in which he supported the dispersion of mobile small rebel groups and opposed the concentration of a regular army that had been the preference of Zachariadis. He also advocated as an alternative to the pursuit of conciliation with the State and the termination of the Civil War. However, Zachariadis went also to USSR and received promises from Stalin to support the DA with airplanes and cannons. Shortly before the orders from Moscow were to cease the Civil War, Zachariadis managed to persuade Stalin to change his mind, so that the DA struggle could be extended for a few more months. Finally, Markos was permanently left aside from the administration of the DA, as well as from the Greek mountains, in the accusation of the «right opportunist deviation». Zachariadis, Vladas, Bartziotas, Karagiorgis, and Gousias participated in the Supreme War Council and undertook the general command as «Commander-in-Chief»!

On the 26th of August 1948, the Supreme War Council decided to be placed next to the DA General Administration. The Council would exercise KKE's control over the operations that was headed by the General Headquarters. Chief of the Supreme War Council was appointed (by himself!) N. Zachariadis. The exclusion of M. Vafiadis from the leadership caused the removal of the Executives who were close to him, as his friend General

---

[5] Partsalidis was a former MP and Major from Kavala

Kikitsas. Moreover, Chrysa Hatzivasiliou, a prominent member of the KKE also disappeared for years from the KKE's affairs as being ill, and the obsolescence of K. Karagiorgis began. In the summer of 1948, there were still a few groups with communist guerrillas throughout mountainous Greece, but their main volume was restricted in Agrafa, Western Macedonia and Epirus. After the loss of Grammos, discussions went on in the high ranks of the DA.

In June 1948, Zachariadis rejected Tsaldari's proposal for peace by making a statement that he would accept a ceasefire only if he «*judged the members of the government*»! At that time Markos called for a truce.

Naval operations

On the 6th of September 1948 the Commander of the patrol ship, P. Spyromilios, «The Warrior», neutralized a small boat from which ammunition was disembarked to the south of Leonidio. It was then found that the commander of the vessel was Albanian, despite that the crew consisted of Greek guerrillas and he had the task of bringing supplies from Durres to Peloponnese. Since then, the naval surveillance of the coasts of Western Greece and Peloponnese was increased.

The attacks in towns continue

As already mentioned, the guerrillas use to attack various towns in order to suppress the morale of the citizens, to get supplies and to recruit men and women. In Sparta and Naoussa, they attacked and managed to control temporarily the towns, leaving many victims behind. These occupations were accompanied by a lot of rioting, and hence the KKE leadership was forced to write for these: «*they have been unpopular acts that hurt us politically»*. The guerrillas used to take a lot of supplies from the towns that they temporarily occupied, but they had the problem of moving them to the mountains that they controlled. The guerrilla attacks cost a lot of losses which could not be replaced.

The attack of Karditsa

On the 11th-12th of December 1948, K. Karagiorgis, the former Director of the newspaper Rizospastis, as the Head of 4,000 men with two Divisions and Captains Giotis, and Diamantis (Giannis Alexandrou), attacked and dominated Karditsa after a bloody battle. On the 13th of December, as they were leaving, they took supplies and compulsorily recruited young men, women, and children; forty citizens were killed in the city.

EVENTS OF 1949

General Papagos the absolute leader

The appointment of A. Papagos as the Chief of the NA was the subject of thought and debate for quite some time, but it was finalized on the 11th of January 1949. He then immediately organized the action plans of the NA on a new basis. Instead of defending, he took the initiative to move and began generalized attacks on assembled guerrillas in mountainous Thessaly as well as in mountains Grammos and Vitsi. In January 1949, the Socialists Svolos and Tsirimokos with a patriotic announcement stated their position and condemned the concessions made by the KKE to the Slavs against the integrity of Greece. On the 20th of January 1949, the Greek government was politically enlarged at the request of the United States. S. Venizelos and

S. Markezinis were appointed to help Prime Minister Sofoulis, who was weak because of his advanced age.

The attack to the town of Naoussa

The attack to Naoussa was led by Gousias and it was launched on the evening of the 11th January 1949, with 2,500 guerrillas, thus taking control of some fortified hills with strategic importance. The defenders were about 1,000 people with the proper equipment and several armed citizens who remained in strongholds and being either neutralized or had escaped and recruited those they could. The injured Captain Agamemnon Gratsios (who in 1975 became Chief General of the staff) transferred to 424 Military Hospital of Thessaloniki. The Lanaras factory was set on fire. The guerrillas looted and refilled with clothes, boots, and weapons. Many of the so-called «reactionaries», e.g. not communists, were executed while about 400 young people were forcibly recruited. The NA had difficulty entering the city because of mines and ambushes.

On the 14th of January 1949, the invaders left Naoussa to prevent themselves from being trapped. Many buildings were destroyed by the guerrillas and the atrocities that happened, and they are written in some anti-communist books, are indescribable. The rebels also suffered many casualties, particularly from air attacks as they were leaving the city. Several of the violently recruited men had the chance to escape. The losses of the DA were comparable to the NA ones, but the price for the communists was more, because it was difficult to be replenished.

The attack on Karpenisi

On the 21st of January 1949, the leader of the DA KGANE K.

6. The Civil War 1946-1949

Karagiorgis (his real name was Giftodimos) gave instructions to attack Karpenissi. Captain Giotis (Charilaos Florakis), together with Captain Diamantis (i.e. two divisions) and many others participated in this attack. The operation began at night and after a battle that lasted until 15:00, the guerrillas finally dominated the city. The heavy snow blocked streets completely and prevented the NA from attacking immediately to liberate the city. Then Papagos demanded that MP Pausanias Katsotas, (the former Commander of the 1st Brigade of El Alamein), should be reinstated. Thus, Katsotas got promoted as Supreme General headed by the Supreme Military Administration of Middle Greece, and he started advancing with the NA to Karpenissi. The very heavy snow though eventually suspended temporarily the movement of the Katsotas Units. Tsakalotos arrived with difficulty in Evritania, met Katsotas and they planned together to regain Karpenissi.

The guerrillas, however, had taken the money out of the banks, executed prominent dissidents, even entire families, destroyed public buildings, ripped off various supplies of food and clothing that they could carry with them. They had also taken over 100 mules, very useful as a means of transport, and violently recruited many young people. Many right-wing fugitive inhabitants of the city died because of the cold weather. Eventually, the city was free after 20 days. Immediately afterward a 120-car convoy arrived at Karpenissi with food and other supplies, along with the Minister of Provision Welfare Konstantinos Karamanlis.

The guerrilla forces fled also to Agrafa and in March began to climb to Epirus. However, their attempt to attack Arta failed. Then, the Brigade of Diamantis' guerrillas was sent to Roumeli. It was unsuccessfully attacked at Lidoriki but the Commander of Livadia, Brigadier General Markopoulos, was captured and executed.

The attack to Florina

On the 12th of February, the DA's under the leadership of Gousias failed to invade Florina. The experienced General Nicholas Papadopoulos (his nick-name «grandfather», was given by his men) resisted and the DA had many casualties there. The losses of the battle of Florina were terrifying; from the NA side, 4 officers and 40 soldiers were killed, 13 officers and 207 soldiers were injured, while two officers and 33 soldiers were missing; from the DA side 783 men were dead and 350 of them were captives, 200 of them were captured, when a DA's Brigade managed to penetrate the city, but got surrounded. The impact of the Battle of Florina was significant; it was a great victory for the NA that cost a lot in the DA as far as men and it added to the moral of the NA's men.

The dates of the main DA's attacks in cities are summarized in table 5.

Tracking guerrillas of KGANE

After the departure of the guerrillas from Karpenissi, the A' Division started the persecution of the Karagiorgis forces in the framework of the plans «ROCKET» and «HUNTER». The men of Captain Giotis and Diamantis, suffering from mourning and starving, became an easy target for the attacks of the A' Army Corp of the NA and suffered greatly in fights on the 21st-24th of March 1949. The remnants of the two DA's Brigadiers finally managed to hide in Agrafa. Tsakalotos and Papagos were strongly tangled and they exchanged letters for the issue of the future tactics of the war, despite the fact that a few days before Papagos congratulated Tsakalotos. Van Fleet visited Tsakalotos and prompted for peace with Papagos.

6. The Civil War 1946-1949

Table 5. Attacks of the communist guerrillas in cities and towns

12/2/1947	Aridaia*	9/3/1948	Gortynia
13/2/1947	Sparta*	12/3/1948	Kalavryta
19/5/1947	Florina	5/4/1948	Diakofto
29/5/1947	Florina	7/4/1948	Komotini
29/5/1947	Kilkis	11/4/1948	Kalavrita
25/6/1947	Metaxades	26/6/1948	Zacharo
13/7/1947	Kastoria	18/7/1948	Karditsa
28/7/1947	Grevena	28/7/1948	Polygyros
21/9/1946	Deskati*	22/8/1948	Aegio
18/10/1947	Metsovo*	30/8/1948	Dimitsana
25/10/1947	Giannitsa	5/9/1948	Tyrnavos
21/10/1947	Edessa	14/9/1948	Ayia
14/11/1947	Komotini	29/9/1948	Larissa
25/11/1947	Amaliada	13/10/1948	Zacharo
7/12/1947	Soufli	3/11/1948	Chrysoupolis
8/12/1947	Atalanti	20/11/1948	Ptolemaida
31/12/1947	Ypati	15/12/1948	Konitsa
23/1/1948	Aegion	12/12/1948	Karditsa*
10/2/1948	Thessaloniki	22/12/1948	Naoussa
23/2/1948	Githio	11/1/1949	Naoussa*
2/3/1948	Anchialos	21/1/1949	Karpenissi*

Note: Asterix indicades a temporary success.

Tactical battles; the role of Tito

Zachariadis' decision to engage in battles was decisive to the outcome of the war against the DA. Besides, the limitation of the DA control within only two mountain ranges, Grammos and Vitsi, and the evacuations of the villages near the border reduced the possibilities of further forced recruitment for manpower. It also created conditions of a tactical but not guerrillas war. Finally, Tito's closure of the borders came in the summer of 1949. Until then, the Croatian Dictator helped Zachariadis' men with supplies, care of wounded, as well as military training in the special camp that existed in Bulkes. The Head of the Camp of Bulkes M. Pechtasidis, was a nephew of Ioannidis' wife, and had created a communist police-legalized community. He fanatically chased the dissenters with informers, forced interrogations and tortures. In total, 95 guerrillas, victims of Pechtasidis and indirectly Zachariadis were murdered in Bulkes. Eventually, Pechtasidis was murdered by a man of Zachariadis. On the 8th of February 1948, a meeting of the leaders of Yugoslavia and Bulgaria with Stalin took place. Stalin said to them that the struggle of the KKE in the mountains has no likelihood of success. He added that «Greek and Yugoslavs communists live in a deep illusion and with their picks, they create political difficulties for all of us». The Greek communists had then to be crumpled; that is «Svarnut» in the Russian language.

The maneuver of Grammos

In the autumn of 1949, the men and women of the DA made an adventurous sudden movement in Grammos. Without being noticed due to the heavy fog, 5,500 guerrillas went in the rear of the NA men. Thus, they easily within 25 days recaptured many positions that the NA had occupied for which much blood was spilled in 1948: «Prophet Elias» «Fourkas», «Giphtissa», «Tabouri», «Stratsanis Tower». Much less was remaining of the Vitsi fortress.

The strong A´ Arm Corp of the NA started to operate in May and the two Divisions of Captain Giotis and Diamantis were persistently under persecution. However, KGANE now had only 3,500 - 4,000 men compared with the 30,000 men of the opposing NA, and the guerrillas were in a precarious state of

6. The Civil War 1946-1949

fatigue and hunger. In the first half of May, their army had been dissolved by many dead men, captive or deserters. Diamantis was killed on the 21st of June 1949, while the leader of the Cavalry Brigade Stefas, committed suicide along with his wife before they were captured. The men from the local Headquarters under Koligiannis moved to the General Headquarters in Grammos, but only about 250 DA's men survived. The National border closed shortly in 1949

Since 1947 the DA had been staffed and renewed only by violent recruitment of peasants. Markos wrote that «only 10% were volunteers by 1947». The issue of the DA's reserves had become unresolved and therefore the participation of women, even young girls aged 16-17, had been considerably increased in both auxiliary and combat services. In the spring of 1949, women accounted for 30% of the DA's combat power and 70% of its auxiliary groups.

General Grigoropoulos leading the C´ Army Corp was operating in all the border areas of Central and Eastern Macedonia as well as in Thrace. The guerrillas in mountains Kaimaktsalan, Vermio, Beles, Agistro, and in general in the entire area of Metaxa's fortress, were eliminated. In the various clashes, the guerrillas retreated for their security, crossing the borders of Bulgaria. The C´ Army Corp has made numerous small movements, sometimes defending and sometimes attacking small guerrilla groups. The difficulty in eliminating the guerrillas was that in every difficult case they would cross the borders. The action of the NA in the Civil War in January 1949 had always been successful, except for the capture of Naoussa (three days) and Karpenissi (twenty days). In the spring of 1949, the aid from Yugoslavia was virtually stopped and only the guerrillas were allowed to move freely from the borders. However, on the 5th of May, Tito decided and closed the border even for the guerrillas. This meant that neither men nor aid would cross the Greek-Yugoslav border. Whoever had passed from

Greece to Yugoslavia would be disarmed. Another problem for men of the DA was the lack of food.

On the 24th of June 1949, Sofoulis died in advanced age, having previously succeeded not only as a politician in difficult circumstances but also as a human being. The Deputy Prime Minister Alexandros Diomedis became then Prime Minister succeeding Sofoulis. However, the struggle of the NA with the DA seemed to have been rated and was approaching to its end.

Finishing businesses at mountains Grammos and Vitsi on 1949

According to NA calculations in June 1949, around 17,500 guerrillas were operating across Greece. Around 4,000 of them were left at the two historic mountains of the Civil War. The dispersion of the guerrillas was great, and they no longer had their former support from the mountain villages. The ratio of gun-power of NA to DA was 10 to 1. The guerrilla reserves had dried up, especially after the terrible losses they had in their winter attacks against cities. The NA confronted these exhausted rebels with two army Corps (A and B) and a total of about 60,000 men. The main responsibility of the attack would belong to the A' Army Corp of Tsakalotos and would co-operate with the B' Army Corp Division, in which General Manidakis had recently been appointed as the leader. The operations started on the 3rd of August with a misleading attack on Grammos under the name «PYRSOS A». The NA managed to occupy significant mounds. The battles were tough and there were many victims and injuries on both sides. In the end, «PYRSOS A» was a partial success. On the 10th of August Operation «PYRSOS B» was launched with an attack on Vitsi. In the first two days, important positions were reoccupied, such as the Small Lessits, Barno and Tsouka. Two days afterward, and after a tough battle, the infantrymen of Ioannou's Division conquered the Lessits Hill, which was of utmost importance to

6. The Civil War 1946-1949

Vitsi's occupation. The leadership of the DA was afraid of being surrounded and it Zachariadis, Gousias, Vladas, and Bartziotas decided to escape onto Grammos. Of course, for this purpose, they had to pass through Albania. In five days, with operation «PYRSOS B», Vitsi was no longer the hideout of the DA. The final battle then would be given in Grammos and it was named «PYRSOS C».

The DA abandoned in Vitsi 70 guns, 16 anti-aircraft cannons, 115 miles, and 436 machine guns. Obviously, the guerrillas were gone in a harry. Moreover, there were 1,182 dead of the DA's fighters and 637 captives. The NA also had serious losses, but fewer than those of the DA: 256 dead and 1,336 injured. The DA forces in Grammos were then about 7,000. Thus, the last attack was designed to be successful and the NA planned that it would occupy and block the border territory where the escape routes to Albania existed. The great difficulty of the NA soldiers was to overcome the dense minefields; these were dealt with special soil torpedoes. Tsakalotos urged all the heads of the Units to work swiftly so as to avoid losing the timing. Gousias decided to send forces to the border of Slimnitsa and Porta Osman, but his men were attacked and disbanded. In the last battles, the 41st and 61st Brigades were run by Colonels E. Mellios and G. Palandas. The movement of these Brigades was swift and on the 28th of August, the highest peak of Grammos was occupied, while Flambouro had also been conquered. Then, Tsakalotos sent in excitement another harsh order: *«thunder them in the Greek territory»*. On the night of the 28th of August, there were ghostly fires on all the hills. Tsakalotos continued to push his men to block the guerrillas from the Batras crossing to Albania, which was occupied on the evening of the 29th of August. On the night of the 29th of August Zachariadis and General Goussias passed the border, going to Albania. Grammos did not become the tomb of «Monarch-Fascism», as Zachariadis said, but the last and staggering defeat of the DA and the «charismatic» leader of the KKE, who believed that he would successfully establish in Greece a «Leninist revolution» for the establishment of a communist «dictatorship of the proletariat». However, the Democratic State Regime had survived, and for the self-exiled survivors of guerrillas, a new «odyssey» would begin!

On the 30th of August 1949, the war ended with the defeat of the DA's men, and most of the guerrillas fled mainly to Albania and a few to Bulgaria to avoid captivity. Approximately 20,000 Slavophones remained in Southern Yugoslavia, which was named by Tito as the «Federal Republic of Macedonia», and formed the «yeast» of «Slavic Macedonian» (sic) fanatics of 1950 and beyond. The decisions of the 6th Plenary session of the Central Committee of the KKE on the 9th of October 1949, included the following: *«It would be a great mistake if, under the new conditions that were created, the KKE continued to the end the armed struggle that offered no prospect of success and would thus lead to a disaster. It would be the same as repeating the erratic coup of Velouchiotis in 1945 when, following Tito's and his clique's suggestions, he did not discipline the KKE leadership, refused Varkiza's Agreement and wanted to continue the war. Tito then sought to exhaust our Democratic Movement so that for at least 10 years we could not recover. This was then the case for his bosses, Anglo-American Imperialists, Monarch-Fascists, and Tito …It would be a lethal sin if we were to make the mistake, we then had avoided with Varkiza. We would thus deprive our Popular Democratic Movement of all the political advantages that the economic and political impasse of Monarch-Fascism offers us, when the country's major struggles break out and flourish, while the main forces of the DA, despite the Monarch-Fascism success in Vitsi-Grammos, remain intact with the gun next to the foot»!*

Zachariadis' different opinion from Markos Vafiadis regarding the kind of combat that should be preferred is «academic». The communists were condemned to be defeated,

6. The Civil War 1946-1949

because they had the rest of the Greek population against them and above all the Americans had supported the Greek government with unlimited resources. Thus, despite the guerrilla struggle, the communists were eliminated throughout Peloponnese and other places where they had operated with small groups, e.g. the islands. Then, only the two mountains Grammos and Vitsi remained for the fight of large military units, where the NA was the undisputed winner. The KKE organization in Athens, with S. Anastasiadis and C. Hatzivassiliou, did not help the guerrilla affairs for long enough, because they had the opinion that they could improve the position of the KKE in society with a «parliamentary struggle». So, the city's inhabitants did not help to join the DA. Besides, the Civil War was a field of foreign policy for Stalin - Tito on the one hand for the British – and Americans on the other. Interestingly, there were different opinions between British and Americans, small but ultimately inconsistent, while Stalin's differences with Tito were unbridgeable; Tito could not accept that he would be a «satellite» of the USSR and a «subordinate» of Stalin. Despite these international difficulties the KKE had become completely dependent on the USSR and Stalin. This dependence lasted many years after the Civil War; thus, for critical matters, the KKE did not have its own position and had to follow the line that USSR ordered.

Leftists' gathering camps – Makronisos

The communists during the Civil War were imprisoned and tried in case they had committed unlawful actions or been arrested as rebels. Leftists who were organized in the KKE and acted subversively, in the context of the so-called «self-defense», were displaced on islands (as political exiles), unless they signed «a statement of repentance» by which they «repudiated Communism». In these islands of exile, they were usually not confined as prisoners, but they were not allowed to leave the island. They rented houses and their expenses were taken care by their families or the KKE. However, there was a separate camp operated in Makronisos from May of 1947. The idea of the Greek government was to create a camp in a controlled place, where the leftists would be kept as unarmed soldiers, because the state had no trust to give them weapons as soldiers in the fighting National Army during the civil war. The Minister responsible for these unarmed soldiers named them as «sappers». The Makronisos sappers consisted of three Battalions called Special Hellenic Army Battalions (ETO). The A-ETO involved the pure communists, who were not pressured by the guards and they even had the freedom to swim in the sea and do various sports. In the B-ETO there were the unspecified believers of communistic ideology; the C-ETO, sappers were designated for «revival» or «emersion» from communist ideology.

The sappers were working manually to build buildings for the operation of the camp: galley, artillery, headquarters, hospital, hostel, water tank, church, theater, officers' club, refreshment juices factory, but also a residence for the Governor. The island was dry and was very hot in the summer. The water came to the island with carriers and it was generally scarce. It is certain that in the first half of the year there was a camp of unarmed soldiers in Makronissos with relative rigor and exhaustive work under very difficult conditions. As the months were passing and the battles in the mountains were thrilling and there were some successes of the guerrillas, several violent acts started taking place in the camp, and the sappers suffered from severe atrocities. The heaviest torture was to order men to carry stones from a point near the sea to a hill and to bring them down without a purpose; naturally, they carried also stones for the works being done. The guards of the Unit Police were carrying bamboo clubs to beat unruly soldiers. The most violent guards were the «revitalized» left-wingers who showed exaggerated enthusiasm to prove their «transformation»!

6. The Civil War 1946-1949

The unarmed sappers of the C-ETO, accepted propaganda against Communism, the so-called «moral education», and it was demanded from them —by exercising psychological and physical violence— to make the «statement of repentance and renunciation of Communism». This statement, however, would isolate them socially from their comrades. Moreover, they received the contempt of the communists who had not accepted to sign such a statement. Those who signed a declaration of repentance had to send detailed letters to their relatives, community presidents and newspapers with charges against communism. After 1948 some political prisoners, former ELAS' officers, various displaced leftists in other islands, and those captured in preventive arrests, such as those carried out by generals Tsakalotos and Pentzopoulos, were exiled to Makronisos and formed the 4th Makronisos Battalion (D-ETO). Moreover, young penitentiaries were transferred to Makronisos. At the beginning of August 1947, the Athens Army Prisoners (AAP) were transferred to this island too. Since then, and until the reformation regime of sappers was abolished, AAP had restricted hundreds of political prisoners who had suffered mainly psychologically as well as physical torture to «recover». Approximately 1,200 civil exiled women were also transferred from Trikeri to Makronisos in January 1950.

The left literature refers extensively to the tortures in Makronisos, which were certainly done; but possibly was an exaggeration regarding the tough behavior, which was then established as the regular military tactic. It was for example reported as the universal haircut and the picking off the thistles from the ground as torture. The behavior of officers, the sergeants, and guards in Makronisos became more arbitrary and violent following the assault by the guerrillas in Konitsa in late December 1947. Since January 1948, the visiting hours were forbidden. The hardening of behavior towards the Makronesian sappers at the beginning of 1948 caused counter-actions by them. On the 29th of February, serious incidents occurred in the A-ETO area because the sappers did not obey the orders of the guards. Actually, the sappers even the sick ones were pressed by the guards to be present in the speech of a priest. In fact, a transfer of about 700 sappers from the A-ETO to the C-ETO was planned. This transfer was the cause of the episodes because the remaining tough communists of the A-ETO did not accept the order and they counteracted. Thus, disobedience to a religious speech was only an excuse. The episodes evolved and the A-ETO men attacked with stones against some officers and, according to the administration, they attempted to disarm and hit the tough Lieutenant Kardaras, while the guards of the Unit Police and some low-rank officers first shot in the air, but eventually aimed at the rebellious sappers. Leftist writers reported that the attack was pre-arranged and unprovoked.

The casualties of the 29th of February 1948 incident was five dead and many more men injured. The following day, the rebellious sappers of the A-ETO organized a funeral while the command of the camp reacted. The next morning on the 1st of March the Commander of Makronisos, Colonel Bairaktaris, was approached with a naval patrol boat near the coast and from the loudspeaker asked the sappers to obey his orders. After a warning and several minutes of wait, during which the rebels did not obey and were throwing stones, the guards began to shoot against the rebels. Several suppers retreated or jumped into sea proceeding to the ship, while the patrol shot at them. On the 2nd of March 1948, the DA's newspaper wrote that «*the Monarch-Fascist Garrison in Makronisos murdered the prisoners of the army leading to death 17 and to injure 61 soldiers*». These figures are consistent with Athenian newspapers of the same date. On the 3rd of March 1948, «Eleftheria» a center-left-wing newspaper and «Empros» a right-wing newspaper, stated that «*31 guards were injured, 155 protesters were arrested, 17 rebels killed, and 40 tramps were injured, while 21 others were slightly injured and remained on*

6. The Civil War 1946-1949

the island. From the C-ETO 3 Lieutenants, 2 seargents and 26 guards from the recovered leftists were injured». However, the newspapers did not report that the rebels were shot by the patrol (inaccuracy, censorship, lack of information or exaggerations of other sources?). A trial of the rebels followed a military court: 114 people were arrested, and severe sentences were given, such as five the death penalty, but no executions were carried out; however, 42 people out of the accused signed a declaration of lawfulness and were released. At that time, the 693 men out of the 700 who were transferred to C-ETO and had been the cause of the episodes signed a declaration of loyalty. The percentage of Makronisos leftists that it was thought to have changed their political beliefs or recovered according to camp officers was important. General Zafiropoulos reported that 15,400 out of a total of 27,770 men fought in the NA against the DA. A Battalion (no 596) was formed by recovered leftists from Makronissos and his men fought valiantly in the mountains of Western Macedonia against the guerrillas, and even conquered an important hill. Of the 1,100 captive left officers, only 100 lost their position rank because they remained as resistant communists. A lot of books have been written about Makronisos by leftist writers, and it is certain that some of them exaggerated, thus it is difficult to trace the truth. Certain sappers or prisoners were tortured, and even some deaths are reported from causes such as internal bleeding, acute peritonitis, etc. The question of whether tortures caused such situations, or they were due to natural causes cannot be ascertained today.

The guards' and certain officers' behavior towards the sappers, inclusion in isolation (barbed wire constructions), beatings and various torture, in order to obtain acceptance of the signature of a «national declaration» and the «renunciation of communism» was brutal, as reported from leftists' writers. In the years of Makronisos, some unjustified deaths occurred in two sappers as a result of torture, as well as some suicides.

Strangely enough for the strict climate of the camp, visits were allowed, few days off were given, there were musical choirs, theatrical performances and boxing matches were organized. Especially, in the A-ETO where the men were unrepentant communists, there was a very calm situation in a scandalous way for the troubled men in the other two battalions, particularly in the C-ETO. Many politicians visited the island, as well as Queen Frederica with King Paul, an event that the famous Greek composer Mikis Theodorakis has referred to with a humorous spirit writing that *«Frederica upset the men with her femininity»*. Moreover, celebrities like writers, poets, musicians, academics passed through Makronisos as prisoners or political prisoners. Makronisos ceased to operate a few years after the end of the civil war.

The Slavophone Greeks in the civil war

The Slav-Macedonian National Liberation Front (SNOF) was founded in November 1943 by Greek Slavophones who were members of the KKE. But after six months of life, when their aims seemed to harm the image of EAM-ELAS, the leaders of the KKE decided the dissolution of the SNOF. Captain G. Giannoulis together with other patriots of ELAS chased many Slavophone soldiers in 1943 and soon the SNOF movement was dismantled. Two battalions of SNOF's men crossed the border, were well accepted in South Yugoslavia by Tito who had the ambitious plans to include the Macedonia the northern territory of Greece to a future multinational State. These two battalions were against the Albanian Nationalists of the Balli Kombetar Organization. On the 30th of April 1945, the Slavophones of Greece formed the Skopje-based People's Liberation Front (NOF), which had political dependence on the communist regime of the «People's Democratic Republic of Macedonia», a federal state in the southern part of Yugoslavia. Must be noted that NOF from Skopje had also a rivalry with the

6. The Civil War 1946-1949

Grekomans of Macedonia in the northern part of Greece and with the Bulgarian Slavs.

On the 14th of October 1946, the KKE and the Communistic Party of Yugoslavia agreed to join the NOF in KKE's rebel army, as well as its participation in the collective bodies of the KKE. In general, several Slav-speaking Greeks participated in the Civil War. This was to some extent due to the geography of the war, but it was also favored by the fact that the KKE and Tito were wishing the autonomy or the integration of Macedonia to Yugoslavia. At some stage of the Civil War, military formations were created exclusively by Slavophones. In 1948, about 45% of the guerrillas were Slavophones, and in the summer of 1949, they reached almost 70% of the guerrillas according to publications of Marantzidis and Kolliopoulos. However, most Slav-speaking or bilingual fighters were neither educated, nor communists, they did not have a conscious Marxist ideology, and hence many of them ended up deserting the fight. The Slavophones were not easily promoted, and they felt underprivileged compared with the Greek leaders of the DA. On this issue, Yugoslavian Prime Minister A. Rankovic complained to P. Roussos, who had the title of the Minister of Foreign affairs of the KKE government in the mountains. After Tito's approach to the USA, many Slavophone fighters were considered to be suspects of Titoism.

On the 10th of July 1948, the KKE issued a decision to agree with the Cominform (Stalin's creation), and all the elements of the NOF leadership would be dropped. This decision led to the split of the NOF, as many of its Executives began to organize the NOF fighters but also to blame the KKE for betraying the struggles of the «Macedonian people». The 5th Plenary session of the Central Committee of the KKE in 1949, decided to support the creation of the «Independent Aegean Macedonia»! This was a late maneuver of Zachariadis to take on board the Slavophones. This decision on the 30th-31st of January 1949 proclaimed: *«In Northern Greece, the*

Macedonian people (he obviously meant the Slavophone Greek citizens living in Greek territory of Macedonia) *gave everything for the struggle and fought with heroism and self-sacrifice that deserves admiration. There must be no doubt that as a result of the DA victory, and the popular revolution, the Macedonian people will find their complete national rehabilitation, as they want it, offering their blood today so as to make it happen».* This political change of Zachariadis was a real turning point against Tito, in favor of Bulgaria, and served the political opposition of the USSR to Tito. On the 27th of March 1949, communist representatives met at the 2nd NOF Conference and decided unanimously to establish their own organization with organizational autonomy yet being part of the KKE, the communist organization of Aegean Macedonia.

When Tito differentiated from Stalin, the KKE took the position in favor of the latter, and hence the army of the KKE lost its support from Yugoslavia. Moreover, the DA's Slav-speaking men also became suspects of having been Revisionists. Thus, in interviews with Slav-speaking men after the Civil War, they often used the phrase «*many locals joined the guerrillas to be saved*», apparently meaning that they were hunted by men of other armed groups; this happened either because they were communists or because they were Slavophones and therefore suspected of cooperating with Bulgarians. Tito's dispute with the USSR had created a crisis between the NOF and the KKE. The NOF had begun to promote the desertion of men of the KKE and therefore replaced its head Keramitzis, because he was favoring Tito, and the NOF's Secretary Paschalis Mitrovski. Moreover, the Slavophone guerrillas did not trust the commander of the 18th Vaina Brigade, who was the only Slavophone with high rank in DA, because his father was a Makedonian fighter of 1904-1908, hence a Grekoman. About 10% of the guerrillas who followed the KKE without any objections were Grekomans. In 1945 Tito

6. The Civil War 1946-1949

designed and implemented the establishment of the «People's Democratic Republic of Macedonia» in the province of Vardarska, naming Skopje as the Capital. There, the development of the «Internal Revolutionary Organization of Macedonians» aiming to the creation of a single independent state of the «Slav-Macedonians» of Greece, Yugoslavia, and Bulgaria was founded. Tito's policy was balanced between:
a. the incorporation of Macedonia of Pirin (belonging to Bulgaria) to Skopje;
b. the creation of an independent single Macedonia which was the pursuit of the EMEO;
c. the creation of a Balkan Slavic Federation.

The USSR observed Tito's «acrobatics» with interest and did not interfere until the latter was weaned completely out of custody. The Tito's effort then was to turn the Slavophones into «Macedonians» and acquire a new Macedonian National identity. In this direction, the names that ended in «of» were changed to «ski», processed the language with Serbo-Croatian additions of scholar elements and promoted «Slavomakedonian historical nationalism» (supposedly descendants of the ancient Macedonians, Aegean, etc. that was absolutely a great historical lie).

The slavophone Greek citizens in many cases they moved outside the country (mainly went to Yugoslavia or Bulgaria): a. After the Greek victory against Bulgaria in 1913, b. after the end of the great war in 1917, c. after the end of the German occupation of Greece in 1944 and d. after the end of civil war in 1949. These men or their descender relatives were and are the most fanatic about Macedonian issues supporting that they are «Macedonians» related to Alexander the Great! Of course, that is impossible because the Slavs came to the Balkan peninsula 1000 years after the era of King Alexander. All educated people in Europe considered this theory as rubbish but the Southern

Slavs continue their propaganda about the «Slavic Aegean Macedonia».

Mass kidnapping of children by the KKE

Due to the increased needs of the DA in manpower, young children 15-16 years old were recruited and after a short-term training, they were equipped and sent to the battles. Thus, young people and teenagers were proportionally the most guerrillas killed. On the 7th of March 1948, the «Provisional Democratic government» of Zachariadis announced its decision to send children to the eastern countries. According to G. Manoukas, who was then responsible for childhood management: *«fear prevailed in those days, and everyone thought. ...By now, the older kids and girls have been taken and were made rebels; now they want the little ones too!»*. The promises of the KKE enlighteners were: *«we will save the children from certain death; paradise life awaits them where they will go; we will soon be liberated, and the children will be returned safely»*. Thus, small children 5-15 years old were taken from their families and they were sent to the Socialist countries, mainly Albania, Bulgaria, Yugoslavia, Hungary, Poland, and Czechoslovakia. Many children came from revolutionary families, but parents were not always in favor of their children's recruitment. In addition, some children were snatched while they were asleep, which seemed to be an easy method because they did not cry! The so-called aim of the DA was supposedly to protect these children from the war, but, in fact, it was basically aiming to educate fighters through a communist education, as shown by their training program. Professor Petros Kokkalis was Minister of Health, Welfare, and Education in the KKE Provisional Government on the mountain and therefore responsible for the health and education of these children. Thus, the aim to educate children was: *«Children have to conquer Marxist art and science, to assimilate the experience of rebuilding socialism and to cultivate the spirit of*

6. The Civil War 1946-1949

internationalism and proletarian solidarity, to become ready and worthy, to rebuild Greece as well».

It is estimated that the DA received 28.000 children according to various sources. According to a statement by Milosevic on the 4th of May 1950 in a Geneva meeting of the Executive Committee of the International Red Cross: *18,500 of the seized children were living in concentration camps in Bulgaria, Romania, Hungary, Czechoslovakia, Poland, Germany and Albania, and 9,506 in Yugoslavia.* During their hikes, often having no footwear, thousands of children suffered from hunger, cold and stress in the mountains. Testimonies indicate that some children died or were lost on the road. Older children attempted to escape and return to their homes, but only a few succeeded it. In Bulgaria in 1949, 88 out of 400 camp boys were selected to be sent back to the mountains to participate in the fight, even though many of them were under the age of 14. This KKE action negates its argument that they were taking the kids to protect them from war; probably, they were taking them to be used in the war and of course to impregnate them with communist ideology.

About 1,000 to 2,000 of those children returned and fought in Grammos and Vitsi after being trained in special camps. The Greek state had made many protests in International organizations and reacted rapidly within the country. Queen Frederica was actively involved and contributed to the organization of 53 child wards, where children of villagers were housed, educated and lived in a safe environment until the end of the war. A smaller number of child-care centers remained operating after 1950 because many of these children were orphaned. More than 2,000 orphaned children were adopted by Greek Americans. Writers of communist ideology consider this event as a scandal; however, since the children were orphaned, these adoptions could ensure their future.

Expiatory victims of the failures of the DA

Zachariadis, after his defeat, commissioned the 7th Division of Thrace to implement the policy of *«weapon close to foot»* in conjunction with guerrilla operations on Greek territory *«as means of pressure on Monarch-Fascism»*. However, this was not easy, there were some runaways, and hence Zachariadis offered as an excuse for the total failure of the DA to have a network of traitors −enemy agents− especially in the 7th DA Division; but in his view, this network had eroded all other Units of the DA. Then, investigations began with tortures, initially in Greek territory and later in Bulgaria under the general supervision of Vladas. Many men and women were accused and tortured, while some of them confessed what they were asked because they preferred to be sentenced to death to stop being tortured. After all these tortures, many men were acquitted, but 32 people lost their lives and some became disabled. Zachariadis and his close leadership group were responsible for executions of fighters, even without a trial. Those who were officers before the war or reserve officers from the time of ELAS, did not have the confidence from the communist leaders, despite the fact that they fought bravely. Among those executed were Brigadier G. Giannoulis, Brigadier G. Georgiadis and Major A. Tsoukopoulos, (their grades are mentioned as they were in the DA hierarchy).

Goussias accused Giannoulis of deliberately retreating in the attack of the National Army in the stronghold of Kamenik. However, the majority of Giannoulis' guerrillas were all exterminated and, in general, the Brigade had a much-reduced composition. On the 20th of August 1948, Giannoulis was assassinated from the rear while sitting on a rock by a man of Gousias. According to all trusted testimonies, no military court was preceded. Of course, the great expiatory victim would be Markos Vafiadis; but he had been very cautious, and perhaps this was the reason that he avoided the execution.

6. The Civil War 1946-1949

The guerrillas of the DA in «Popular Democracies» and the USSR

Zachariadis, Ioannidis, Partsalidis, Bartziotas fell into Albanians' disgrace because a. refused to work as refugees in construction work; and b. refused to support the Albanians with drugs, clothing, and boots that the DA had in its warehouses, on the excuses that *«We ought first to get approval from those who had given us the equipment»,* i.e. to the Eastern European countries and Yugoslavia. There was then increasing hostility between the KKE and the Albanian communist party, so it was decided to send Greek refugees from Albania to other countries of Eastern Europe. However, men and women were found elsewhere, because men moved as military Units, while children were another big issue, and hence for years, family members were looking for each other. Later, special Committees were set up, which recorded 60,000 «refugees» outside Greece, of whom 48,000 lived in the eastern European countries (USSR's satellites) and 12,000 in Tashkent of the USSR. About 25,000 of this population were from children that guerrillas had already sent outside of Greece.

The deleterious effects of the civil war

The Civil War had many victims —dead and injured— on both sides. The DA had most of the losses, in total 38,221 dead, while the NA had 8,440 deaths. It seems that the victims of the Civil War were many times more than the victims of the war with Italy and Germany.

The KKE for a quarter of a century remained out of the law and the former guerrillas lived for many years in the countries of «real socialism» (Eastern Europe and the Soviet Union), where only a communist party was allowed to function within the proletariat's dictatorship. Many DA men were transferred to Tashkent, Uzbekistan, where a large internal division of the KKE

would later develop. In 1955 and 1962, in Tashkent and other cities, the disputes of the «Orthodox» communists emerged, who had the support of the KKE, with the KKE Revisionists and evolved into assaults and destruction of households, and assassinations even with stabs. As a result of these differences, the KKE was divided into two separate parties in 1968:
a. The KKE (without any further definition) and
b. The KKE of the «Interior». The names were due to the fact that the «Orthodox KKE» was totally dependent on the outside, i.e. the Soviet Union, and people called it «the Foreign KKE», thus indicating the dependence of this Party to Stalinism. However, the USSR leaders now were against Stalin's ideas (the most prominent among them was Nikita Khrushchev).

Among the victims of the Civil War, they were also the communists who were sentenced to death (guerrillas, OPLA's men, former militaries) and the killings in 1943-1944 as well as the Dekembriana losses, or the killings from the anti-communist organizations, e.g. hunting groups, and the Organization X.

Table 6.
Dead in the Civil War Yearly according to state data

Year	NA		DA
	officers	soldiers	Mixed dead from guerillas
1946	13	113	836
1947	104	1011	7629
1948	330	3909	16382
1949	190	2579	13373
1050	14	177	201
Total	651	7789	38421

Table 7.
Wounded men in the Civil War per year according to Greek military authorities

Year	NA officers	NA soldiers	DA Mixed dead from guerillas
1946	6	186	unknown
1947	165	2770	unknown
1948	834	14474	unknown
1949	664	9945	unknown
1050	39	413	unknown
Total	1708	27788	unknown

Table 8.
Number of communists sentenced to death 1945-1948 and killed by shooting, includes the numbers of deaths and executions in the years 1945-1948

Year	From Military Court	From Criminal Court
1945	0	9
1946	116	0
1947	688	79
1948 (until 31/8)	742	143
Total		231

(Source: S. Grigoriadis, in History of Contemporary Greece; Volume 5).

A precondition for the Civil War was the existence of «social hatred». This was cultivated by the communist «guidance» and «enlightenment». There have been a lot of factors on both sides that had been raised over the years. State authoritarianism «blew oxygen to the flame» of Communism, and imprisonments and displacements were increasing the general feeling of injustice. The German Occupation gave the opportunity to KKE, on the pretext of National Resistance, to organize the planning for an armed conquest of power after the Germans would depart. The political-military chessboard was mixed with Britain, the USSR, and the United States. Greece was the convenient experiment and it was in a vicious circle on the backdrop of the «cold war» of the two opposing blocks: the Free World and the countries of «real Socialism».

For many years certificates of social beliefs were used for the Greek citizens. Thus, someone had to have the right papers so that he could be appointed to the state. For many years after the civil war ended, the leftists were not able to become officers in the army and could not enter the Military Schools. Moreover, for many years the institution of displacement in the islands had been operating. The secret reports of policemen had reached in 1962 up to 60,000. Political prisoners in camps and prisons at the end of 1951 were approximately 17,000 and progressively declined to 1,665 by spring 1962. However, soon no one would be left in prison for his political beliefs.

The exile of the Caucasian Pontians

While the DA guerrillas reached the limits of their resistance to the mountains, farther in the Soviet Union in the evening of the 13th of June 1949, Stalin's Secret Police surrounded the villages of Caucasian Greeks and forced them to leave their homes and to enter trains with which they were moved to central Asia near the USSR borders with China. There, they used them as slaves in forced labor, and many of them died from exhaustion, poor nutrition, and bad weather. Some of the displaced persons were executed on the grounds that they were «enemies of the people» and that Trotskyists sought to establish an autonomous Pontian State with conspiratorial organizations. At the same time, some Greek communists were exterminated with similar categories and methods. Stalin,

6. The Civil War 1946-1949

although he signed the UN human rights provisions, brutally tortured the Caucasian Pontians and added them to his millions of victims.

Criticism after the War

D. Vladas, who worked as a Chief of Staff in the Civil War Committee, wrote for Siantos: *«Siantos has always been a provocateur and, in my opinion, a UK Intelligence Service agent. Thus, he was able to play its role in beating down the National Resistance Movement into the Occupation and then into the December adventure. He played a double game by serving both English and Soviet interests following the Churchill-Stalin agreement».*

Several accusations were also spelled out regarding Zachariadis, which were only made public after the change of views on the USSR and the fall of Stalinism (de-Stalinization and later perestroika). Most of those who accused him eventually formed the core of the «KKE Interior» party. Paul Nefeloudis stated in his book on the Sources of Evil Deception: *«In any case, from all the facts known to date, the conclusion that comes out is that the Soviet Union sacrificed Greece, the epic of its Resistance against the occupiers and the Greek communist Movement, on the altar of serving its general interests (the exchange with Poland's borders), and in the name of subjugation of the Party to the revolution».* It must be noted that the evolution of KKE's leaders after the Civil War was rather sad, even tragic. Most of them were struck by their political inconsistencies; others returned to Greece miserably after an amnesty, and others were marginalized in the countries of «real Socialism». Zachariadis, aged 70, was restricted as a home prisoner exiled to Surbkut of Siberia where he committed suicide, in 1973 by hanging.

The Greek state proved to be very generous, as it gave pensions to all of the guerrillas who returned to Greece, although they had no enough working years in our country and they had been tried to abolish the bourgeois state, fighting very hard against it in a civil war.

EPILOGUE

Greece, apart from the human losses during the war 1940-1941, suffered a lot during the triple occupation of their country by Germans, Italians, and Bulgarians. The resistance of Greek people during the foreign occupation was multiple: sabotages against trains, ships, and bridges; information about the German army that was sent to British in Cairo and attacks to the enemy's small units or isolated soldiers and officers. However, the cost of this resistance was very high. Many Greeks were executed, and many villages were burned by the conquering forces. The cost for Greece was huge and disproportional to the benefit of the allies.

On the other hand, concerning the resistance of left organizations (EAM-ELAS), it soon seemed that the main aim of them was the domination of postwar Greece using the arms. The civil conflicts during Occupation and the fights of Dekembriana were followed by the 1946-1949 civil war that had cost a lot of human lives and a great delay in Greece's economic development. The KKE-DA equipped by communistic countries (mainly Yugoslavia) was at one side proclaiming classes' detestation and on the other side was the Greek state with the rest of the people. While all European countries after the end of the war tried to build up their economy and built up their infrastructure, Greece was spending forces and was losing people during a bloody civil war. I believe that the knowledge of the history of the three rounds of Greek civil war could be beneficial in the future evolution of Greek political affairs.

When the communist dictator Josef Broz Tito's in 1945-1946 established the «Socialist Federal State of Macedonia», the USA immediately considered this a lie and fraud. It is a sad thing that nowadays prevailed an agreement (that signed at

Lake Prespa in June 2018) which has been considered by the European Unity and the USA as good and beneficial to peace and cooperation in the Balkans. This agreement was considered unacceptable by the majority of Greek people (Huge demonstrations and a large number of resolutions and publications and polls). The truth is that Macedonia was liberated from the Turkish occupation in 1913 and then is an indisputable part of the Greek state in Northern Greece. In the state of Skopia there is a mix of ethnicities, such as southern Slavs speaking a mixture of Bulgarian and Serb language, while about 30% of their population is Albanian.

I am sure that in the end, the truth will prevail. There is only one Macedonia —located within the Greek territory— and the name Macedonia has been Greek since antiquity. It is unacceptable that this historical and cultural name to be stolen by another country.

LITERATURE

*During the writing of the above text,
I had in mind the following publications*

Αβέρωφ-Τοσίτσας Ε. *Φωτιά και τσεκούρι.* Εκδ. ΕΣΤΙΑΣ, Αθήνα 1976.

Αλιβιζάτος ΝΚ. *Οι πολιτικοί θεσμοί σε κρίση, 1922-1974: Όψεις της ελληνικής εμπειρίας.* Εκδ. Θεμέλιο, Αθήνα 1986.

Αναγνωστόπουλος ΝΑ. *Παράνομος τύπος κατοχής.1941-1944.* Αθήνα 1960.

Ανδριώτης ΝΠ. *Το Ομόσπονδο κράτος των Σκοπίων και η Γλώσσα του.* Εκδ. Τροχαλία, Αθήνα 1992.

Αντιφασιστική Δημοκρατική Ένωση. *Πρακτικά της δίκης της στενής αυτοάμυνας ή ΟΠΛΑ Θεσσαλονίκης.* Θεσσαλονίκη 1947.

Αντωνίου ΚΣ. *Ιστορία της Ελληνικής Βασιλικής Χωροφυλακής 1933-1967.* Εκδ. Λαδιάς Γ., Αθήνα 1967.

Αντωνίου Γ. και **Μαραντζίδης Ν**, (Επιμελ). *Η εποχή της σύγχυσης. Η δεκαετία του '40 και η ιστοριογραφία.* Εκδ. Εστία, Αθήνα, 2008.

Αντωνόπουλος Κ Ε. *Εθνική αντίσταση 1941-1945.* Αθήνα 1964.

Αξελός Κ., *Για μας δεν υπήρχε ιερό και όσιο.* Συνέντευξη στον Κ. Κορνάτη. Χρόνος, Τεύχος 6, Οκτώβριος 2013.

Αποστολάτος Γ. *Η παγίδευση της ιστορίας.* Αθήνα 2006.

Αρχηγείον Βασιλικής Χωροφυλακής. *Δράσις χωροφυλακής κατά την περίοδον 1941-1950.* Τυπογραφείο Β.Χ., Αθήνα 1962.

Βακαλόπουλος ΓΔ. *Διλοχία κυνηγών. Στα κρησφύγετα του «Καπετάν Γιώτη».* Εκδ. Λόγχη, Αθήνα 2011.

Βαφειάδης Μ. *Απομνημονεύματα. 1940-1944.* Τόμος 2. Εκδ. Νέα Σύν-ο-ρα, Αθήνα 1985.

Βαφειάδης Μ. *Απομνημονεύματα. 1945-1949.* Τόμος 3. Εκδ. Νέα Σύνο-ρα, Αθήνα 1985.

Βελλιάδης Αννίβας. *Γερμανική πολιτική διοίκηση στην κατεχόμενη Ελλάδα 1941-1944.* Εκδ. Ενάλιος, Αθήνα 2008.

Βλαντάς Δ. *Ο Ζαχαριάδης και 22 συνεργάτες του.* Εκδ. Γλάρος, Αθήνα 1984.

Βλαντάς Δ. *Εμφύλιος πόλεμος 1945-1949.* Εκδ. Γραμμή.

Βοβολίνης ΚΑ. *Μυστικές εκδόσεις.* Εκδ. Ν. Αλικιώτη, Αθήνα 1945.

Γαρουφαλιάς ΔΕ. *Κείμενα και αναμνήσεις από τον τραγικό Δεκέμβριο του 1944.* Αθήνα 1981.

Γκανάτσιος-Χείμαρρος Β. *Ανιχνεύοντας τις ρίζες της ήττας. Επανεκτιμήσεις και παρελειπόμενα για τον εμφύλιο και τα Μετεμφυλιακά.* Εκδ. Επίκεντρο, Θεσσαλονίκη 2011.

Γκατζογιάννης Ν. *Ελένη.* Εκδ. Economia Publishing, Κέρκυρα 2012.

Γκητάκος ΧΜ. *Δεκεμβριανά 44.* Εκδ. Μέτρον, Αθήνα 1997.

Γονατάς Στ. *Απομνημονεύματα 1897-1957.* Αθήνα 1958.

Γρηγοριάδης Σόλων. *Ιστορία της σύγχρονης Ελλάδας 1941-1974.* Εκδ. Polaris, Αθήνα 2009, 2010 και 2011.

Δασκαλάκης Α. *Ιστορία βασιλικής χωροφυλακής.* Αθήνα 1973.

Δέλτα ΠΣ. *Νικόλαος Πλαστήρας.* Ερμής ΕΠΕ, Αθήνα 1979.

Δήμα-Δημητρίου Α. *Η πολιτικοστρατιωτική κατάσταση στην Ευρώπη και τα Βαλκάνια πριν την κήρυξη του ελληνο-ιταλικού πολέμου.* Στρατιωτική Επιθεώρηση Σεπ.-Οκτ. 2008.

Δημητρίου Δ. (Νικηφόρος) *Αντάρτης στα βουνά της Ρούμελης. Χρονικό 1940-44.* Αθήνα, 1978.

Δημητρίου Δ. (Νικηφόρος). *Ελληνική Εμπειρία 44-67.* Αθήνα, 1971.

Δημητρίου Δ. (Νικηφόρος). *Δεκεμβριανά 1944, 2ο Σύνταγμα του ΕΛΑΣ. Παγίδευση και αφοπλισμός και η συνεχιζόμενη προς τα χείριστα ελληνική τραγωδία (1941-1997).* Αθήνα 1997.

Δημητρίου Πάνος. *Εκ βαθέων. Χρονικό μιας ζωής και μιας εποχής.* Εκδ. Θεμέλιο, Αθήνα 1997.

Δρακούλης Μάξιμος. *Τα οικογενειακά του ΚΚΕ.* Αθήνα 1949.

Δρίτσιος Θωμάς. *Γιατί με σκοτώνεις σύντροφε;* Εκδ. Γλάρος, Αθήνα 1983.

Literature

Πανελλήνια συνομοσπονδία εθνικών αντιστασιακών οργανώσεων. *Εθνική αντίσταση των Ελλήνων 1941-1944.* Αθήνα 2001

Εμφύλιος πόλεμος: *Ιδεολογικός ή ξενοκίνητος επιβουλή;* Εκδ. «Ιστορικά ντοκουμέντα». Τεύχος 3 Νοέμβριος 1975.

Ενεπεκίδη Π.Κ. *Η Ελληνική Αντίστασις 1941-1944 όπως αποκαλύπτεται από τα μυστικά αρχεία της Βέρμαχτ εις την Ελλάδα. Μια νεοελληνική Τραγωδία.* Εκδ. ΕΣΤΙΑ, Αθήνα 1964.

Ζαούσης Αλ. *Η τραγική αναμέτρηση. 1945-1949. Ο μύθος και η αλήθεια.* Εκδ. Ωκεανίδα, Αθήνα 1996.

Ζαούσης Αλ. *Ο Εμπαιγμός. 21 Απριλίου 1967 - 24 Ιουλίου 1974.* Εκδ. Παπαζήση, Αθήνα 1997.

Ζαφειρόπουλος ΔΓ. *Ο αντισυμμοριακός αγών. Αθήνα 1945 - 1949.* Αθήνα 1956.

Ηλιάδου-Τάχου Σ. *Μέρες της ΟΠΛΑ στη Θεσσαλονίκη. Τα χρώματα της βίας (1941-1945). (Μέσα από το αρχείο του Ν. Τσιρώνη)* Εκδ. Επίκεντρο, Θεσσαλονίκη 2013.

Η Εμπόλεμη Ελλάδα 1940-1949. *Εις Ιστορία του Νέου Ελληνισμού 1770-2000.* (Τόμος 8). Συλλογικό έργο. Εκδ. Ελληνικά Γράμματα, Αθήνα 2003.

Ηλιάδου-Τάχου Σ. *Από τη Βάρκιζα στο Μπούλκες. Διαδρομές ζωής ή θανάτου.* Εκδ. Επίκεντρο, Θεσσαλονίκη 2014.

Ηλιόπουλος ΗΙ. *Ιωάννης Μεταξάς ο Εθνικός κυβερνήτης.* Εκδ. Δημοκρατικός Τύπος ΑΕ, Αθήνα 2016.

Ηλιού Φ. *Ο ελληνικός εμφύλιος πόλεμος. Η εμπλοκή του ΚΚΕ.* Εκδ. Φιλίστωρ, Αθήνα 1999.

Η στρατιωτική δικτατορία 1967-1974. Συλλογικό έργο. Επιμέλεια Καραμανωλάκης Β. Εκδ. ΤΑ ΝΕΑ, Αθήνα 2010.

Ήφαιστος Π, Κουλιόπουλος Κ, Χατζηβασιλείου Ε. (επιμ.). *Η έναρξη του ψυχρού πολέμου, 1941-1950: Στρατηγικά ή ιδεολογικά αίτια.* Ινστιτούτο Διεθνών Σχέσεων, Πάντειο Πανεπιστήμιο, Αθήνα 2012.

Ιατρίδης ΓΟ. *Η Ελλάδα στη δεκαετία του 1940. Ένα έθνος σε κρίση.* Εκδ. Θεμέλιο, Αθήνα 1984.

Ιστορικό λεύκωμα. *Ελευθέριος Βενιζέλος.* Κείμενα Παπαδάκης ΝΕ και Γαρδίκα-Κατσιαδάκη Ε. Εκδ. Το ΒΗΜΑ, Αθήνα 2016.

Ιωαννίδης Γ. *Αναμνήσεις. Προβλήματα της πολιτικής του ΚΚΕ στην Εθνική Αντίσταση 1940-1945.* Εκδ. Θεμέλιο, Αθήνα 1979.

Καβαλά Μαρία. *Η Θεσσαλονίκη στη γερμανική Κατοχή (1941 –1944). Κοινωνία, οικονομία, διωγμός Εβραίων.* Διδακτορική διατριβή. Επιβλέπουσα Έφη Αβδελά. Πανεπιστήμιο Κρήτης, Ρέθυμνο 2009.

Καλλιγά Α. *Φλεγόμενη Πολιτεία. Η μάχη της Αθήνας.* Εκδ. Μαρής Κοροντζής, Αθήνα 1946.

Καλογρηάς Βάιος. *Το αντίπαλο δέος. Οι εθνικιστικές οργανώσεις αντίστασης στην κατεχόμενη Μακεδονία (1941-1944).* University Studio Press, Θεσσαλονίκη 2012.

Καλύβας Σ. Ν. *Καταστροφές και θρίαμβοι: Οι 7 κύκλοι της σύγχρονης ελληνικής ιστορίας.* Εκδ. Παπαδόπουλος, Αθήνα 2015.

Καλύβας Σ. και **Μαραντζίδης Ν.** *Εμφύλια Πάθη. 23 ερωτήσεις και απαντήσεις για τον Εμφύλιο.* Εκδ. Μεταίχμιο, Αθήνα 2015.

Κανελλοπούλου Ευγ. (επιμ.). *Ελληνικά Ολοκαυτώματα 1940-1945.* Εκδ. Λιβάνη, Αθήνα 2010.

Καπετάν Μαύρος (Νίκος Χατζηνικολάου). *Ταραγμένα Χρόνια στον Νέστο. Κατοχή, Αντίσταση, Εμφύλιος.* Επιμέλεια Σπύρος Ρούλης. Εκδ. Νιραγός, Θάσος 2008.

Καραγιάννης Γ. **1940-1952.** *Το δράμα της Ελλάδος, έπη και αθλιότητες.* ΕΝΑ-ΙΔΕΑ. Αθήνα.

Καραγιάννης Χ. *Η προδομένη Αντίσταση 1941-1950.* Εκδ. Εθνικού Συνδέσμου Ελασιτών Μακεδονίας-Θράκης. Θεσσαλονίκη 1962.

Καράγιωργας Γ. *Η ΟΠΛΑ χωρίς Θρύλο.* Εκδ. Δωδώνη, Αθήνα-Γιάννινα 1997.

Καράμερος ΓΔ. *Το Μακεδονικό Ζήτημα.* Γ΄ εκδ. Αθήνα 1953.

Καραποστόλης Β. *Διχασμός και εξιλέωση. Περί πολιτικής ηθικής των Ελλήνων.* Εκδ. Πατάκη, Αθήνα 2010.

Καργάκος ΣΙ. *Από το Μακεδονικό Ζήτημα στην εμπλοκή των Σκοπίων.* Εκδ. Gutenberg, Αθήνα 2003.

Literature

Καργάκος ΣΙ. *Η ελληνικότητα της Μακεδονίας.* Εκδ. Ομάδα Πρωτοβουλίας για την προάσπιση του ονόματος της Μακεδονίας, Αθήνα 2006.

Κόκκινος Κ. *Τα χρόνια της κρίσης 1942-1945.* Εκδ. Ι. Σιδέρης, Αθήνα 1979.

Κολλιόπουλος ΙΣ. *Λεηλασία φρονημάτων.* Εκδ. Βάνιας, Θεσσαλονίκη 1995.

Κολλιόπουλος ΙΣ. *Ιστορία της νεωτέρας Ελλάδος. 1797-1980.* Εκδ. Βάνιας, Θεσσαλονίκη 2014.

Κόντης Β. *Σοσιαλιστικά κράτη και ΚΚΕ στον εμφύλιο πόλεμο.* Εκδ. Επίκεντρο, Θεσσαλονίκη 2012.

Κόντης Β και Σφέτας Σπ.(επιμ.). *Εμφύλιος πόλεμος. Έγγραφα από τα γιουγκοσλαβικά και βουλγαρικά αρχεία.* Εκδ. Παρατηρητής, Θεσσαλονίκη.

Κοραντής Ι. *Πολιτική και Διπλωματική Ιστορία της Ελλάδος (1941-45).* Εκδ. Εστία, Αθήνα 1987.

Κοσιώρη ΙΑ. *Το χρονικό της Εθνικής Αντιστάσεως Πελοποννήσου 1941-1945.* Αθήνα 1992.

Κουβάς Σωτ. *Η ιστορία του ΚΚΕ,*(δεν αναγράφονται λοιπά στοιχεία).

Κούλογλου Στ. *Μαρτυρίες για τον εμφύλιο και την ελληνική Αριστερά.* Εκδ. ΕΣΤΙΑΣ, Αθήνα 2005.

Κύρου Άδ. *Χρονικόν 1940-1944. Εθνική αντίσταση και εθνική μειοδοσία.* Αθήνα 1982.

Κύρου Αχ. *Η Νέα Επίθεσις κατά της Ελλάδος. Το Ελληνικόν Πρόβλημα ενώπιον του Ο.Η.Ε. (Ιανουάριος 1946-Δεκέμβριος 1948).* Εκδ. Αετός, Αθήνα 1949.

Κύρου Αχ. *Η συνωμοσία εναντίον της Μακεδονίας.* Εκδ. Αετός, Αθήνα 1950.

Κύρου Αχ. *Η αποφασιστική καμπή του πολέμου.* Εκδ.Αετός, Αθήνα 1946.

Κύρου Ηλίας Ι. *Μακεδονία και βόρειοι γείτονες.* Εκδ. Κυρομάνος, Θεσσαλονίκη 1993.

Λαζαρίδη Δημ. *Ευτυχώς ηττηθήκαμε σύντροφοι.* Εκδ. Πελασγός, Αθήνα 2003.

Λαζαρίδου Μ. *Πόλεμος και αίμα.* Εκδ. ΕΜΕΙ, Αθήνα 2010.

Λάμπρου Χαρίτων. *Οι Τσάμηδες και η Τσαμουριά.* Αθήνα 1949.

Λεονταρίτης Γ.Α. *Η αλήθεια για τα Δεκεμβριανά.* Εκδ. Μέτρον, Αθήνα 2007.

Λιναρδάτος Σπ. *Από τον εμφύλιο στη χούντα.* Εκδ. Παπαζήση, Αθήνα 1977.

Μαθιόπουλος Β. Π. *Ο Δεκέμβριος του 1944,* Εκδ. Νέα Σύνορα-Α. Λιβάνη, Αθήνα, 1994.

Μαθιόπουλος Β. *Η Ελληνική Αντίσταση 1941-1944 και οι Σύμμαχοι.* Εκδ. Παπαζήση, Αθήνα 1977.

Μαλτέζος Γερ. *ΔΣΕ. Δημοκρατικός στρατός Ελλάδας.* Αθήνα 1984.

Μανούκας Γ. *Παιδομάζωμα. Το μεγάλο έγκλημα κατά της φυλής,* Αθήνα 1961.

Μαραντζίδης Ν. *Γιασασίν Μιλλέτ: Ζήτω το έθνος: Προσφυγιά, κατοχή και εμφύλιος: Εθνοτική ταυτότητα και πολιτική συμπεριφορά στους τουρκόφωνους ελληνορθόδοξους του δυτικού κόσμου.* Επιμέλεια σειράς: Καλύβας Σ. Ν. Πανεπιστημιακές Εκδόσεις Κρήτης, Ηράκλειο 2001.

Μαραντζίδης Ν. *Δημοκρατικός στρατός Ελλάδας.* 1946-1949. Εκδ. Αλεξάνδρεια, Αθήνα 2010.

Μαραντζίδης Ν, Τσίβος Κ. *Ο Ελληνικός Εμφύλιος και το διεθνές κομμουνιστικό σύστημα.* Εκδ. Αλεξάνδρεια, Αθήνα 2012.

Μαρίνος Θεμ. *Ο εφιάλτης της Εθνικής Αντίστασης.* Εκδ. ΕΜΕΙΣ, Αθήνα 2003.

Μαρκεζίνης Σπ. *Σύγχρονη πολιτική ιστορία της Ελλάδος 1936-1975.* Εκδ. Πάπυρος, Αθήνα 1994.

Μαρκοβίτης Μ. *Όχι δεν είμαι εχθρός του λαού.* Εκδ. Επίκεντρο, Θεσσαλονίκη 2017.

Μέρτζος Ν Ι. *Τα δέκα θανάσιμα αμαρτήματα του Κ.Κ.Ε. Επίσημα κείμενα,* 3η έκδ. Εκδ. Ι. Σιδέρης, Αθήνα 1985.

Μέρτζος ΝΙ. *Μακεδονικό. Το μήλον της έριδος Βουλγαρίας – Σκοπίων.* Εκδ. ΕΜΣ, Θεσσαλονίκη 2013.

Μέρτζος ΝΙ. *Σβαρνούτ. Το προδομένο αντάρτικο.* Εκδ. Ερωδιός, Θεσσαλονίκη 2005.

Literature

Μέρτζος ΝΙ. *Αρμάνοι Βλάχοι φύλακες της Μακεδονίας.* Εκδ. Δ. Κυριακίδη, Θεσσαλονίκη 2014.

Μεταξά Λέλα. *Το ημερολόγιο της ομηρίας μου 1944-1945.* Αθήνα 1989.

Μιχαηλίδης ΙΔ. *Τα πρόσωπα του Ιανού. Οι ελληνογιουγκοσλαβικές σχέσεις την περίοδο του ελληνικού εμφυλίου πολέμου (1947-1949),* επιμέλεια σειράς Ευάνθης Χατζηβασιλείου. Εκδ. Πατάκη Αθήνα, 2007.

Μουμτζής Σάκης. *Η κόκκινη βία. 1943-1946. Η μνήμη και η λήθη της αριστεράς.* Εκδ. Επίκεντρο, Θεσσαλονίκη 2013.

Μουμτζής Σάκης. *Η κόκκινη βία. 1947-1950. Ένοχες σιωπές αριστεροί μύθοι.* Εκδ. Επίκεντρο, Θεσσαλονίκη 2015.

Μπαρτζιώτας ΒΓ. *Εξήντα χρόνια κομμουνιστής.* Εκδ. Σύγχρονη Εποχή, Αθήνα 1986.

Μπόλαρης Λέανδρος. *Αντίσταση, η επανάσταση που χάθηκε: Με παράρτημα για τους Τροτσκιστές του Β΄ Παγκόσμιου Πολέμου.* Εκδ. Μαρξιστικό Βιβλιοπωλείο, Αθήνα 2012.

Μπουγάς ΙΚ. *Ματωμένες μνήμες 1940-45.* Εκδ. Πελασγός, Αθήνα 2010.

Μυριδάκης Μ. *Αγώνες της φυλής. Η Εθνική Αντίστασις ΕΔΕΣ-ΕΟΕΑ 1941-1944.* Αθήνα 1948. Εκδ. Σιδέρη Ι, Αθήνα 1976.

Μυριδάκης Μ. *Οι 4 γύροι του ΚΚΕ.* Εκδ. Σμπίλιας, Αθήνα 1988.

Νάτσινας Αλ. *Συμπεράσματα και παρατηρήσεις επί του διεξαχθέντος εν Ελλάδι αγώνος κατά των Κ/συμμοριτών. Τακτική αντιμετωπίσεως ανταρτικών δυνάμεων.* Θεσσαλονίκη 1951.

Νικητόπουλος Γ. *Η δίωξη των δοσιλόγων της Κατοχής στην Πάτρα.* Διδ. Διατριβή. Πάντειο Πανεπιστήμιο. Αθήνα 2007.

Νικολαΐδης Κ. *Ετυμολογικόν λεξικόν της Κουτσοβλαχικής γλώσσης.* Εκδ. Π. Α. Σακελλαρίου, Αθήνα 1909.

Νικολακόπουλος Η, Ρήγος Ά, Ψαλλίδας Γρ. *Ο εμφύλιος πόλεμος: από τη Βάρκιζα στον Γράμμο, Φεβρουάριος 1945-Αύγουστος 1949.* Εκδ. Θεμέλιο, Αθήνα 2002.

Νικολακόπουλος Η. *Η καχεκτική Δημοκρατία. Κόμματα και εκλογές 1946-1967.* Εκδ. Πατάκης, Αθήνα 2001.

Ξανθόπουλος Νίκος. *Ποίος έπταισεν; Εμφύλιος 1941-1944*. Εκδ. Αφών Κυριακίδη ΑΕ, Θεσσαλονίκη 2013.

Οικονομίδης Φοίβος. *Η επανάσταση στην Ελλάδα, το ΚΚΕ και οι ξένοι φίλοι, Εμφύλιος 1945-1949*. Εκδ. Λιβάνης, Αθήνα 2011.

Παπαγιάννης Σ. Α. *Τα παιδιά της λύκαινας. Οι «επίγονοι» της 5ης ρωμαϊκής λεγεώνας κατά τη διάρκεια της Κατοχής (1941-1944)*. Εκδ. Σοκολής, Αθήνα 2004.

Παπαθανασίου Τρ. Χ. *Η μαύρη βίβλος των εγκλημάτων του ΕΑΜ*. Εκδ. Ελεύθερη Σκέψις, Αθήνα 2011.

Παπαϊωάννου Αχ. Ι. *Ο Κρόνος τρώει τα παιδιά του*. Εκδ. Μπίμπης, Θεσσαλονίκη 2013.

Παπαϊωάννου Αχ. Ι. *Η παρέλαση των γιγάντων*. Εκδ. Μπίμπης, Θεσσαλονίκη 2008.

Παπαϊωάννου Αχ. Ι. *Η διαθήκη του Ν. Ζαχαριάδη*. Εκδ. Γλάρος, Αθήνα 1986.

Παπακωνσταντίνου ΘΦ. *Ανατομία της επαναστάσεως. Οι τρεις γύροι του ΚΚΕ*. Αθήνα 1952.

Παπαχελάς Αλέξης. *Ο βιασμός της ελληνικής Δημοκρατίας*. Εκδ. ΕΣΤΙΑΣ, Αθήνα 1997.

Πασχαλίδης Ν. *Ο Βρετανός διοικητής Nicholas Hammond*. Εκδ. Σφακιανάκη Κ., Θεσσαλονίκη 1995.

Πετζόπουλος Θ. 1941-1950. *Τραγική πορεία*. Αθήνα 1953.

Πικρός Γ. *Το χρονικό της Μακρονήσου*. Εκδ. Δρόμων, Αθήνα 2013.

Πυρομάγλου Κομνηνός. *Ο Δούρειος Ίππος*. Εκδ. Δωδώνη, Αθήνα 1978.

Ροδίτσας Ν. *Τα χρόνια της κρίσης 1946-1949*. Αθήνα 1981.

Σαμουήλ Γ. *Η εποποιία του Μακρυγιάννη*. Αθήνα 1950.

Σαραντόπουλος ΚΑ. *Βαλτέτσι 1944. Μαρτυρία*. Εκδ. Αρμός, Αθήνα 2003.

Σαράφης Στέφ. *Ο ΕΛΑΣ*. Εκδ. Επικαιρότητα, Αθήνα 1999.

Σαράφης Στέφ. *Μετά τη Βάρκιζα*. Εκδ. Επικαιρότητα, Αθήνα 1979.

Literature

Στάικος Μακρής Πέτρος. *Ο Άγγλος πρόξενος. Ο υποπλοίαρχος Noël C. Rees και οι βρετανικές μυστικές υπηρεσίες: Ελλάδα - Μέση Ανατολή (1939-1944).* Εκδ. Ωκεανίδα, Αθήνα 2011.

Στίνας Α. *ΕΑΜ-ΕΛΑΣ-ΟΠΛΑ.* Εκδ. Διεθνής Βιβλιοθήκη, Αθήνα 1984.

Συλλογικό έργο. *Ελληνική Πολιτική Ιστορία 1950-2004.* Εκδ. Ελληνικά Γράμματα, Αθήνα 2009.

Συλλογικό έργο. *Οι άλλοι καπετάνιοι.* Επιμ. Ν. Μαραντζίδη. Εκδ. ΕΣΤΙΑΣ, Αθήνα 2006.

Σφέτας Σπ. *Όψεις του μακεδονικού ζητήματος στον 20ό αιώνα.* Εκδ. Βάνιας, Θεσσαλονίκη 2001.

Σφέτας Σπ. *Ελληνοβουλγαρικές αναταράξεις 1880-1908: Ανάμεσα στη ρητορική της διμερούς συνεργασίας και στην πρακτική των εθνικών ανταγωνισμών.* Εκδ. Επίκεντρο, Θεσσαλονίκη 2008.

Σφέτας Σπ. *Η διαμόρφωση της Σλαβομακεδονικής ταυτότητας: Μια επώδυνη διαδικασία.* Θεσσαλονίκη : Βάνιας, 2003.

Σφήκας ΘΔ. *Με τον Μέτερνιχ ή με τον Πάλμερστον; Οι Βρετανοί και ο Δεκέμβριος του 1944.* Εκδ. Ζήτη, Αθήνα 2015.

Σφήκας ΘΔ. *Πόλεμος και ειρήνη στη στρατηγική του ΚΚΕ 1945-1949.* Εκδ. Φιλίστωρ, Αθήνα 2001.

Σφήκας ΘΔ. (επιμ). *Το σχέδιο Μάρσαλ. Ανασυγκρότηση και διαίρεση της Ευρώπης.* Εκδ. Πατάκης, Αθήνα 2011.

Τολούδης Πέτρος. *Νίκος Ζαχαριάδης. Το κρυφό αρχείο της εξορίας.* Εκδ. Παπαζήση, Αθήνα 1991.

Τσακαλώτος Θρ. *Πώς εσώθη η Ελλάς. Δεκέμβριος 1944.* Εκδ. Εθνικό Ίδρυμα Αμύνης, Αθήνα 1981.

Τσιρπανλής ΖΝ. *Πώς είδαν οι Ιταλοί τον πόλεμο του 1940-41.* Εκδ. Πανεπιστημίου Ιωαννίνων, Ιωάννινα 1974.

Τσουδερός Ε. *Ιστορικό Αρχείο 1941-1944.* Εκδ. ΦΥΤΡΑΚΗ, Αθήνα 1990.

Τσουκαλά Κ. *Η ελληνική τραγωδία.* Εκδ. Νέα Σύνορα-Α.Α. Λιβάνη, Αθήνα 1981.

Φάκελος Ελλάς 1931-1944. *Τα αρχεία των μυστικών σοβιετικών υπηρεσιών.* Εκδ. Νέα Σύνορα, Α.Α. Λιβάνης, Αθήνα 1993.

Φαράκος Γρ. *Δεκέμβρης του 44. Νεότερη έρευνα, νέες προσεγγίσεις*. Εκδ. Φιλίστωρ, Αθήνα 1966.

Φαράκος Γρ. *Ο ΕΛΑΣ και η Εξουσία*. Εκδ. Ελληνικά Γράμματα, Αθήνα 2000.

Φαράκος Γρ. *Άρης Βελουχιώτης: το χαμένο αρχείο, άγνωστα κείμενα*. Εκδ. Ελληνικά Γράμματα, Αθήνα 1997.

Φαράκος Γρ. *Σχετικά με το ΚΚΕ και το κομμουνιστικό κίνημα*. Ανάτυπο, εκδ. Ελλ. Γράμματα, Αθήνα 2005.

Φροντιστής Αθ. *ΠΑΟ, ιστορία και προσφορά της στην εθνικήν αντίστασιν 1941-45*. Εκδ. Τριανταφύλλου, Θεσσαλονίκη 1977.

Χασιώτης ΙΚ. *Οι Έλληνες της Ρωσίας και της Σοβιετικής Ένωσης. Μετοικεσίες και εκτοπισμοί, οργάνωση και ιδεολογία*. University Studio Press, Θεσσαλονίκη 1997.

Χατζής Θανάσης. *Η νικηφόρα επανάσταση που χάθηκε*. Εκδ. Δωρικός, Γ΄ Έκδ. Αθήνα 1983.

Χατζηβασιλείου Ευάνθης. *ΠΕΑΝ (1941-1945). Πανελλήνιος Ένωσις Αγωνιζομένων Νέων*. Εκδ. Σύλλογος προς Διάδοσιν Ωφελίμων Βιβλίων, Αθήνα 2004.

Χατζηθεοδωρίδης ΒΓ. *Η Κατοχή στην Αν. Μακεδονία-Θράκη (1941-1945)*. Ν.Ε.ΠΟ.Τ.Α. Δράμας 2002.

Χρηστίδης Χ. *Χρόνια Κατοχής 1941-1944. Μαρτυρίες Ημερολογίου*. Αθήνα 1971.

Χρυσάφης Σωτήριος. *Ο Αρμαγεδών του Εμφυλίου: Κιλκίς $4^η$ Νοεμβρίου 1944*. Προσωπική έκδοση. Θεσσαλονίκη 2019.

Χρυσοχόου Αθανάσιος. *Η ελληνοαλβανική συνεννόηση δια την ένωσιν της Αλβανίας με την Ελλάδα*. **Εκδ. Ηπειρωτικής Εστίας Θεσσαλονίκης, Θεσσαλονίκη 1952**.

Χρυσοχόου Α. *Η κατοχή εν Μακεδονία – Η δράσις του ΚΚΕ*. Εκδ. Εταιρείας Μακεδονικών Σπουδών. Θεσσαλονίκη 1949.

Literature

Χρυσοχόου Α. *Η κατοχή εν Μακεδονία – Η δράσις της Βουλγαρικής προπαγάνδας.* Εκδ. Εταιρείας Μακεδονικών Σπουδών. Θεσσαλονίκη 1950-1952.

Χρυσοχόου Α. *Η κατοχή εν Μακεδονία. Οι Βούλγαροι εν Ανατολική Μακεδονία και Θράκη.* Εκδ. Εταιρείας Μακεδονικών Σπουδών. Θεσσαλονίκη 1951.

Χρυσοχόου Α. *Η κατοχή εν Μακεδονία. Η δράσις της Ιταλορουμανικής προπαγάνδας.* Εκδ. Εταιρείας Μακεδονικών Σπουδών, Θεσσαλονίκη 1951.

Hondros J.L. *Occupation and resistance. The Greek agony, 1941-1947,* Pella Publishing Company, Αθήνα 1983.

Ξένων συγγραφέων

Close DH. (Επιμέλεια). *Ο Ελληνικός Εμφύλιος πόλεμος 1943-1950. Μελέτες για την πόλωση.* Εκδ. Φιλίστωρ, Αθήνα 1996.

Close DH. *Οι ρίζες του εμφύλιου πολέμου στην Ελλάδα.* Μετάφραση Ρένα Χρυσοχόου. Εκδ. Φιλίστωρ, Αθήνα 2003.

Eudes D. *Οι καπετάνιοι. Ο ελληνικός εμφύλιος πόλεμος 1943-1949.* Εκδ. Εξάντας, Αθήνα 1974.

Hammond NGL. *Δυτική Μακεδονία, αντίσταση και συμμαχική στρατιωτική αποστολή 1943-1944.* Εκδ. Παπαζήση, Αθήνα 1990.

Hampe Roland. *Η διάσωση της Αθήνας τον Οκτώβριο του 1944.* Εκδ. Πορεία, Αθήνα 1994.

Hamson Denys. *We Fell Among Greeks.* Ed. Ace Books, London 1957.

Jordan S. William. *ΕΑΜ. Η αλήθεια για το ελληνικό δράμα.* Εκδ. Ελεύθερη Σκέψις, Αθήνα.

Mayer Herman Frank. *Από τη Βιέννη στα Καλάβρυτα.* Εκδ. ΕΣΤΙΑΣ, Αθήνα 2004.

Mayers E. *Η Ελληνική περιπλοκή.* Εκδ. Εξάντας, Αθήνα 1975.

Mazaouer Mark. *Τα Βαλκάνια.* Εκδ. Πατάκη, Αθήνα 2002.

Mazaouer Mark. *Στην Ελλάδα του Χίτλερ. Η εμπειρία της Κατοχής.* Εκδ. Αλεξάνδρεια, Αθήνα 1994.

Mulgan J. *Report on experience.* Ed. MPG Books LTD, London 1947.

Nige Clive I. *Εμπειρία στην Ελλάδα.* (1943-1948). Εκδ. Ελληνική Ευρωεκδοτική, Αθήνα 1980.

Richter Heinz. 1936-1946. *Δυο επαναστάσεις και αντεπαναστάσεις στην Ελλάδα.* Εκδ. Εξάντας, Αθήνα 1975.

Richter Heinz. *Η Εθνική Αντίσταση και οι συνέπειές της.* Εκδ. Ελληνικά Γράμματα, Αθήνα 2009.

Walace David. Βρετανική πολιτική και αντιστασιακά κινήματα στην Ελλάδα. Εκδ. Ωκεανίδα, Αθήνα 2009.

Woodhouse C. *Το μήλον της έριδος.* Εκδ. Εξάντας, Αθήνα 1975.

Woodhouse C. and Clogg R. *The Struggle for Greece, 1941-1949.* London 2002.

www.ingramcontent.com/pod-product-compliance
Lightning Source LLC
Chambersburg PA
CBHW080541220526
45466CB00010B/2992